Family Resorts
of the Northeast

Family Resorts

OF THE NORTHEAST

*Carefree Vacations for All
—Including Mom and Dad*

Nancy Pappas Metcalf

The Countryman Press
Woodstock, Vermont

The Countryman Press, Inc.
P.O. Box 175
Woodstock, Vermont 05091

Library of Congress Cataloging-in-Publications Data

Metcalf, Nancy Pappas, 1948-
    Family resorts of the Northeast : carefree vacations for all,
including mom and dad / Nancy Pappas Metcalf ; photographs by the
author.
        p. cm.
    Includes index.
    ISBN 0-88150-185-9 (pbk.) :
    1. Resorts--Northeastern States--Guide-books. 2. Family
recreation-- Northeastern States--Guide-books. 3. Northeastern
States--Description and travel--1981- --Guide-books.   I.Title.
TX907.3.N95M47   1991
647.947401--dc20   91-8211
                                                              CIP

Printed in the United States of America

10 9 8 7 6 5 4 3 2 1

Cover, text design, and part-title illustrations by Leslie Fry
Cover photograph of Basin Harbor Club by David Lane Roby, Jr.

For Bill Pappas

Contents

Introduction and Acknowledgments

This book got its start a few years back when, after an exhausting and expensive summer week spent cooking and sweeping up in a fancy rental on Martha's Vineyard, we set out to find another vacation option. We vaguely sensed that out there somewhere were resorts that not only welcomed families with young children like ours but also—wonder of wonders—cooked their meals and cleaned their cabins so the parents could have an actual rest.

We eventually found such a place and had a wonderful time. Our search would have been easier if there had been a useful guidebook to northeastern family resorts to consult. Being a writer by trade, I decided to write one.

This guide includes all sorts of family places, from noisy dude ranches to grand mountain resorts to breezy seaside inns to remote lake fishing camps throughout our region. They encompass a vast range in terms of size, amenities, and price. Some are well known; others have never appeared before in any guidebook that I'm aware of. But every one has passed the most rigorous user test of all: a visit by a family with young children.

You will not find any stars or ratings in this book. Rather, I have tried to address the practical questions parents have about a prospective vacation spot. Do the rooms have refrigerators for the baby's formula? Is there a separate sleeping space for the children? Can a young teenager find something fun to do? Is the waterfront safe for a nonswimming preschooler? What does the place look and feel like? What kinds of people will we encounter there?

The resorts were visited over the course of two summers by my own family or by other writers, with their spouses and children. The resorts extended their hospitality with no guarantee from us other than that we'd describe them as fairly and completely as we could.

As with all travel guidebooks, the information in this one is subject to change. Especially in uncertain economic times, resorts can dramatically alter their focus, or even close altogether, with surprising suddenness. The rates and information listed within are current as of this writing, in the fall of 1990. But if you are interested in a place described herein, for heaven's sake call or write for a current brochure and rate card.

This book could not possibly have been researched and written in two summers without the assistance of the following parents and children: Matt, Lori, Jesse, and Ashley Damsker; Bobbie Roessner and Craig, Taylor, and Liam Baggott; Tom, Anne, and Clare Condon; Nancy Polk and Jack and Peter Hasegawa; David, Jill, Ian, Christopher, and Philip Barrett; Steve, Susan, Allison, and Scott Grant; Kathleen Megan and Peter and Nell Pach; Kristina Goodnough and Dan, Alice, and Owen Barrett; George Kriebel and Sarah and Chloe Metcalf; and Mary and Elizabeth Bannon.

Finally, and most importantly, my husband Steve Metcalf, stepdaughter Audrey Metcalf and daughters Laura and Jane Metcalf served as the book's most enthusiastic researchers and supporters. My love and gratitude to them all.

Explanation of rate terms

AP (American Plan)—Lodging and all meals

MAP (Modified American Plan)—Lodging plus breakfast and dinner

B&B (Bed & Breakfast)—Lodging plus breakfast

EP (European Plan)—Lodging only

Grand Resorts

FRY 1991

The Balsams Grand Resort Hotel

Dixville Notch, NH 03576
603-255-3400 or 1-800-255-0600
Open year-round

Lodging: 232 rooms with private bath, telephone; 75 rooms can interconnect as suites.

Rates: $127–$168 per person per day, double occupancy, AP. For children under 18 staying in same room as parents, their age times $6 per night, minimum $24 per night. Rates slightly lower in winter.

Facilities: Billiards room; game room; reading room; TV room; theater-nightclub; cocktail lounge; gift shop; clothes shop; resident craftspersons. Summer—Lake with passenger paddlewheeler, paddleboats, canoes, and rowboats; outdoor pool; 18-hole Donald Ross golf course; 9-hole, par 32 golf course; fly fishing in lake; putting green; 2 trap fields; shuffleboard; croquet; 3 red clay, 3 all-weather tennis courts; volleyball court; badminton courts; bicycle rentals; horseshoes; hiking trails. Winter—12 alpine ski trails with snowmaking; 50 km groomed cross-country trails; lighted outdoor skating rink; base lodge with lunch grill and ski shop; toboggans; snowshoeing; ski instruction.

Family amenities: Playground; nursery at ski area base lodge; supervised summer children's day camp; supervised children's dinner; babysitting with advance reservations; nonalcoholic summer nightclub for ages 12–21.

The swimming pool and 1918 wing.

Photo courtesy of The Balsams Grand Resort Hotel

The Balsams calls itself a "grand resort hotel," and there's no hyperbole involved. This eccentrically glorious piece of architecture, plopped in the middle of a spectacular mountain wilderness, represents resort life as it used to be lived—with discreet, thorough service and so many things to do you couldn't get through them in a month's stay.

Before we visited the Balsams, we figured our kids would be intimidated by such a big, fancy place. Instead they adored exploring its endless public rooms and corridors, and reacted to its elegant, formal dining room by putting on good manners we didn't even realize they possessed. (They were, as usual, unimpressed by the superb food, but that's another story.)

Time was that the White Mountains were studded with big, gracious places like this. One by one, nearly all of them folded or burned down. The Balsams itself went through some hard times. But since the 1970s it's been capably managed by the same four men under a lease from its longtime owner, a rubber magnate named Neil Tillotson. They've poured millions into an ongoing restoration and maintenance program and brought back the Balsams' grand tradition of gracious service. The place earns money now. Its future seems secure.

Probably the most famous thing about the Balsams is its setting— a place in the upper White Mountains known as Dixville Notch. The hotel is surrounded on three sides by mountains and on the fourth by small, perfect Lake Gloriette, with more mountains rising steeply behind it.

The second most famous thing is the building itself, actually two distinct buildings hooked together by a low section containing an entry portico and a tea lounge. The older section, dating from 1866, is a long, sprawling four-story white frame building with a rambling porch, and contains the resort's main public rooms. The "new wing," opened in 1918, is a seven-story brown stucco affair with orange tiles decorating its roof and cupolas.

The public rooms themselves are worth the trip. They go on for what seems like acres of brocaded upholstery, ornate Victorian chairs, settees, tables, floral rugs, and sweeping staircases. All this is the result of recent, skillful, and expensive renovation, but a portly 1910 gentleman with a handlebar mustache and pocket watch would look perfectly at home here.

The rooms themselves are being unobtrusively updated, a few each year. Both old and renovated rooms contain the resort's signature seafoam-blue furniture and ruffled sheer tieback curtains; the updated rooms have somewhat more stylish wallpaper, wicker chairs, thicker rugs, and considerably more modernized bathrooms. About a third of the rooms can interconnect to form suites.

The Balsams maintains a one-to-one employee-guest ratio, meaning there's no service stone left unturned here. You can even hire a staff person to videotape your family pursuing vacation enjoyments.

In recent years the resort has made a concerted bid for families with children in the 5-and-up age range (the absence of infant and toddler programs is deliberate; management believes kids that young would simply disrupt the dining room too much). In the summer kids ages 5–12 have a day camp based in a big ground-floor room that opens directly out onto an elaborate new playscape. With 15,000 acres and princely recreational facilities, there's no dearth of activities. The kids go on hikes, visit a local dairy farm, take conga drum and trumpet lessons from musicians in the hotel ballroom, ride in the boats, or splash in the big lakeside swimming pool (its 3-foot shallow end is fine for the younger nonswimmers). With all this, however, our kids were most deeply impressed with the vintage Coca-Cola vending machine in the playroom, and the daybeds they were allowed to jump on.

The Balsams even makes an effort for adolescents. During the summer season it operates the Cave, a nonalcoholic nightclub specifically for teenagers and young adults. It features rock videos, movies, games, music, and dancing nightly until midnight. The resort's game room also includes 13 video games.

Amazingly, the children's program is free to all American Plan guests. Even more amazingly, so are most of the resort's other facilities. Unlike many luxury resorts, the Balsams does not charge extra for tennis, golf, or ski lift tickets at its private ski mountain a short shuttle-bus ride down the highway.

And we are talking deluxe facilities, too. The resort wasn't kidding when it named the golf course the Panorama: Donald Ross, the legendary Scottish course architect, laid it out in 1912 literally on top of a mountain. From the gorgeous stone-and-timber old clubhouse you can see into Canada and Vermont (American Plan guests can get a chit for lunch here even if they don't golf). The Wilderness ski area, added in 1966, features a roomy and comfortable base lodge-restaurant, a 1,000-foot vertical drop, 12 trails, and snowmaking.

If your kids are old enough to be left alone asleep in their rooms (or old enough to stay up past 9 P.M.), you can take advantage of the

Balsams' active nightlife. Every evening there's a 35-mm feature film shown in the movie theater, music and dancing in either the lounge or the ballroom, and a lecture on topics ranging from natural history to current events. Weekly events include a staff talent show and a "name-that-tune" entertainment.

As befits a full-service resort, the Balsams goes to extraordinary lengths to make its facilities easily accessible to guests. On checking in, you'll find in your room an extensive description of what's offered and how to sign up for it. There's even a blurb from the resort's naturalist, a Ph.D. who conducts excellent daily hikes and who is supervising an archaeological excavation of the resort's ancient garbage dump (you can help dig if you're so inclined).

Though officially in the White Mountains, the Balsams lies far to the north of the region's best-known tourist attractions. It's a good 50-mile drive on two-lane secondary roads, for instance, to the factory outlets of North Conway. So save your sightseeing for another time and place. The Balsams, we promise, won't let you down.

Basin Harbor Club

Vergennes, VT 05491
802-475-2311
Open mid-May–early October

Lodging: 43 hotel rooms in 2 main buildings; 77 cottages sleeping 2–6. All cottages have phones; some have deck, screened porch, fireplace; most have pantry with refrigerator and wet bar.

Rates: $97–$120 per person per day, AP. Lower rates for children sharing accommodations with parents. Lower rates in May, June, September.

Facilities: Pool and lake swimming; 2 Har-Tru and 3 Plexipave tennis courts; 18-hole golf course; nature trails; badminton; croquet; volleyball; shuffleboard; bicycle rentals; canoe, rowboat, outboard, Sunfish, windsurfer rentals; waterskiing; lake tour boat; jogging-exercise trail; gift shop; cocktail lounge. Additional charges apply for golf, tennis, and boating.

Family amenities: Playground and playhouse supervised daily 9 A.M.–1 P.M. for children ages 3–10, lunch included. Supervised children's dinner 6:45–9 P.M. Golf and tennis clinics, volleyball and softball games, table tennis tournaments, video game room for older children. Babysitting available with advance notice.

This is a grand old resort in the comfortable New England style, a place for well-heeled families to relax in well-serviced, unpretentious ease. It begins, as such places do, with a lovely, manicured setting

A guest cottage.

on the eastern shore of Lake Champlain. Most guests stay in the attractive, luxurious country-style cottages that spread out from the inviting old main lodge, with its big veranda and expansive views of Champlain's rocky western shore and the Adirondack Mountains beyond.

The Beach family has run this resort since it opened in 1886, and the family prides itself on the number of guests who return year after year, generation after generation. Three generations of a family may gather on the veranda before dinner, their blue blazers and bow ties and flowery dresses bright against the white clapboard. The children's hair could still be damp from a late-afternoon dip.

As befits a resort that has developed gradually over the years, every guest cottage is different. Some have screened porches, some picket fences. Some border the golf course or tennis courts. Furnishings vary, too, but all the cabins have phones and refrigerators—no TV though, to the grateful relief of many parents.

All the summertime sports you'd expect at a big lakefront resort are here. There's a 6,400-yard, 18-hole golf course, 5 tennis courts, and a very large outdoor pool with 25-yard marked lanes for lap swimmers. There's also a sheltered sandy beach for lakefront swimming. This is the best place for very young children, as the shallow end of the pool is a bit too deep for them. For older children who feel confident in deep water, there's a diving float anchored a bit offshore.

Lake Champlain is a massive body of water, 120 miles long north to south, that offers good fishing (lake trout, northern pike, perch, bass). The club rents canoes, rowboats, outboards, Sunfish, paddleboats, and windsurfers. Inexperienced canoeists will want to hug the shore, for a summer squall or a passing powerboat can kick up some formidable waves on this big lake.

The 700-acre property takes its name from the sheltered cove that serves as its centerpiece. The main lodge and some of the cabins overlook the harbor. Teens and braver adults waterski from the main dock here. The *Dynamyte II,* the club's 40-foot tour boat, leaves the harbor once or more each day carrying guests on sightseeing tours of Lake Champlain.

But make no mistake: this is a place for the well-heeled. It even has its own well-used private airstrip.

The Basin Harbor Club has terrific food, built upon a stock of Yankee classics augmented by more sophisticated fare. A good thing, too, because this full American Plan resort is a long way away from any other restaurants. Breakfast is served in the formal main dining room, a curved space where nearly every table has a view of the harbor or lake. The menu features the usual entrees as well as a daily special, perhaps kippered herring or homemade sausage with country gravy. The waiters circulate with trays of fresh muffins and pastries, all you can eat.

Lunch is served in the Ranger Room, a more informal eating space overlooking the pool and putting green. The offerings include hot entrees and a huge table of salads and sandwich fixings, including, usually, an excellent seafood salad and a variety of marinated vegetable dishes. The kids can always count on hamburgers and hot dogs. Or, if you'd like, enjoy a family picnic, yours for the asking with a night's advance notice to the kitchen.

Back in the main lodge, dinner is the dressiest meal of the day. Men and boys over 12 wear jackets and ties. Entrees range from beef tenderloin to poached salmon, and every menu includes at least one low-fat heart-healthy selection. Wines and liquor are available. Younger children—under age 7 or so—can opt for a supervised table in a nearby room, followed by playtime until 9 P.M. Most kids quickly discover they prefer this to the stately pace and grown-up menu of the big dining room.

Basin Harbor accommodates children in other ways as well. During the summer season, the resort has a supervised children's program daily from 9 A.M. to 1 P.M., including lunch in the Red Mill, a casual dining space near the airstrip. The age limits are 3–10. The activities center around a playhouse with games, books, toys, and an outdoor playground. The schedule might include a nature walk, a hayride, a luncheon cookout, arts and crafts, or a treasure hunt. After the supervised dinner the children's staff frequently shows a suitable movie in the main lodge's viewing room.

For children too young for the playhouse, the resort will secure a babysitter from an approved list that includes both off-duty employees and local residents.

For children older than 10, who tend to resist structured programs, the resort arranges group activities such as golf and tennis clinics, volleyball games, movies, and teen mixers. Youngsters can also gather at the Red Mill, which has video games.

This area of Vermont is rich in family-oriented activities as well. Within day-trip distance are the Shelburne Museum of Americana and the bustling lakeside city of Burlington, with lots of restaurants and shopping opportunities.

Mohonk Mountain House

Lake Mohonk
New Paltz, NY 12561
914-255-4500
Open year-round

Lodging: 281 rooms, most with private bath, many with working fireplace and balcony; 44 rooms connect through baths to form family suites. Some rooms open May–October only.

Rates: Rooms, $174–$339 per night double occupancy, AP. Family suites, $269–$289 per night double occupancy, AP. Children's rates, under 2, no charge; 2–12, $45 per night; over 12, $55 per night when sharing room with parents.

Facilities: Lake swimming beach; boat dock with paddleboats, canoes, and rowboats for rent; 4 red clay, 2 Har-Tru tennis courts; 2 paddle tennis courts; 85 miles of hiking trails in a 7,700-acre nature preserve; lawn bowling; croquet green; horseback trail rides and pony rides; 9-hole golf course; putting green; barn museum and blacksmith shop; fishing with tackle for rent; carriage rides; fitness center with exercise equipment, saunas, group classes, locker room; croquet; basketball; horseshoes; volleyball; shuffleboard; athletic field; gift shop and snack bar; library; board games; coin laundry; dress boutique; flower shop. Winter—35 miles of marked, groomed cross-country ski trails; ski rentals and instruction; cleared ice-skating rink on lake; skate rentals; snow tubing; horse-drawn sleigh rides.

Family amenities: Morning and afternoon supervised recreation programs for children ages 2–4, 5–6, 7–8, 9–12; supervised outings and programs for teenagers; supervised evening activities for ages 5–12, teenagers; early dinner seating for families with children's menu; babysitting available with advance notice.

In recent years praise and recognition have showered down upon the Mohonk Mountain House, which has been designated a National Historic Landmark. Dozens of magazines have written breathlessly of its charms and used its buildings and grounds as backdrops for photo shoots. In this case, the attention is not only richly deserved but long overdue. The Smiley family has been operating this exemplary, luminous resort in the Shawangunk Mountains for 120 years.

You may well have seen photographs of Mohonk. It is a rambling series of connected three- to seven-story buildings put up along the shore of Lake Mohonk between 1879 and 1910 by two Quaker brothers, Dan and Albert Smiley. Some are of stone, some of dark-stained wood, some of painted wood. All are ornate, Victorian, and virtually unchanged from the day they were finished. The same goes for the interiors, which contain enough period woodwork, mantelpieces, and furniture to stock every antiques store for 50 miles around.

The genius of the Smileys is that they have managed to keep this special place a thriving, up-to-the-minute resort without sacrificing or trivializing its nineteenth-century charm. In addition, from the outset—mind you, this was many, many decades before the environmental movement took hold—the family was determined always to preserve the natural landscape surrounding the hotel. The Smileys placed the bulk of their acreage in a forest preserve, to remain forever wild. The happy result is that Mohonk guests have access to some 85 miles of trails cut through 7,700 acres of glorious woods, peaks, ponds, and cliffs. The importance of this is underscored by the fact that the rest of New Paltz, a university town and suburb down in the once-verdant valley, is now choked with cars and hideous shopping plazas.

Without getting into a geology lesson, suffice it to say that the Shawangunks are an impressive pile of rocks. Tall silver cliffs, many with deep clefts and rifts, loom everywhere, including the perimeter of the deep, clean 17-acre mountaintop lake, opened in some ancient geological split.

Everything about this place reflects human caring and professionalism. Mohonk has all the recreational and service facilities befitting a grand resort, kept in perfect repair and well-staffed—a 9-hole golf course, riding stables, clay tennis courts, a permanent croquet court with putting-green surface, a boat dock, etc. The hiking trails are kept in impeccable condition, as are the 100-odd handmade rustic twig gazebos that lurk around every corner.

The programming is also exceptional. For adults and older children Mohonk arranges a series of imaginative theme weeks and weekends, featuring guest speakers and activities. There are programs on hiking, birding, choral singing, word-game-playing, tennis, running, foreign language immersion, cooking, crafts, and chamber music, to name only a few. New in 1990 was a month-long arts festival which used Mohonk's many splendid public lounges for music performances, poetry and play readings, and dance presentations. It is also possible, of course, to visit with no planned agenda in mind.

Meanwhile, younger guests have access to Mohonk's carefully designed children's program, which runs daily in the summer season and during weekends and holidays (including school vacation weeks) the rest of the year. You can enroll your children in any combination of morning and afternoon sessions, at a charge of $7 per child per session.

The programs are based at the Council House, an old frame building a hundred-odd yards from the main hotel. There is a separate room and fenced playground for the youngest group, the Tykes ages 2–4, with a new and well-chosen selection of games, books, toys, and crafts materials. School-age children are subdivided into three groups—the Explorers (ages 5–6), Scramblers (ages 7–8), and Adventurers (ages 9–12)—with progressively more demanding activities. They use a larger Council House room for crafts and rainy-day activities but otherwise spend their days out and about on the grounds, riding ponies, swimming, hiking, sand sculpting, or hunting arrowheads and fossils.

The term "Scramblers" has a special meaning here, for children have to be at least 7 to be permitted on Mohonk's Scramble, a thrilling trail that makes its way over, under, and between a series of immense boulders and split cliffs deposited near the site of the main hotel in some aeons-old cataclysm. Navigating this maze requires good sneakers and the willingness to go on all fours. Frequently children have to be forcibly stopped from spending entire days going up and down the Scramble.

The kids' program also includes a free evening activity from 7:30

The Mountain House and lake.

Photo by Matthew Seaman

to 9 P.M. that can range from a campfire marshmallow roast to a moonlight swim to a game of flashlight tag.

Mohonk is actively experimenting with programs for the always-tricky over-12 crowd. Counselors have organized hayrides, tennis and golf clinics, mixers, and other activities designed to help adolescents get acquainted with one another out of parental view.

Many of Mohonk's recreational facilities are excellent for children. The bathing beach is located a short walk from the hotel, down a flight of stairs cut into a lakeside cliff. Tons of sand have been trucked in to create a surprisingly large beach, with a gently sloping swimming area marked off by ropes, floats, and docks. It is a typically charming spot, with bridges out to two large sunbathing floats decorated by tall gazebos. The lake bottom drops off sharply underneath the floats. Three times a day a lifeguard in a boat accompanies guests who wish to swim the one-eighth-mile distance across the lake.

Just down the hill from the hotel is the Mohonk Barn Museum, a yellow-painted monster built in 1888 and said to be one of the largest barns east of the Mississippi. It houses an exhibit of antiques all once used at Mohonk: horse-drawn surreys, a wicker phaeton with a parasol, a water wagon, bobsleds, an Edison dictating machine, a 1925 Model T, a two-horse treadmill, and innumerable tools. There is also a working blacksmith's shop and regular demonstrations of country crafts.

The guest rooms here are as historically faithful as the rest of the place. To this end, Mohonk takes care to spend its $1 million annual maintenance budget as invisibly as possible. A "redone" room has the same oak Victorian furniture and trim as the original, down to the porcelain pedestal sinks and bathroom wall tiles. What's up-to-date are the newly plastered walls, the modern wiring, the leakproof plumbing, the smooth-running insides of the drawers on the antique oak bureaus. The family suites consist of two rooms, each with a single bed and double bed, connected by a bathroom. Most have at least one working fireplace. The entire complex, which looks like a firetrap, has never had a significant blaze owing to an elaborate system of smoke detectors and sprinklers.

Most meals are taken in the three-story-tall main dining room, in which every surface—walls, floors, ceilings—is elaborately carved unpainted wood. Breakfast, bountiful as per grand resort custom, is served from either a menu or a hot-and-cold buffet. The lunch buffet features an excellent salad bar, cold meats, cheeses, and several hot entrees. In the warm weather families with children are encouraged to lunch at the Granary, an open-air lunch grill near the beach that serves sandwiches, salads, burgers, and the like. That way children don't have to get out of their bathing suits and can be back in the water in no time at all. Box lunches can also be provided if ordered in advance. Dinner is served from a menu in the main dining room. In addition to the usual Continental choices there is always one low-fat, low-cholesterol entree. The first seating, at 6 P.M., includes a children's menu and finishes in time for the evening children's programs.

Mount Washington Hotel and Resort

Bretton Woods, NH 03575
603-278-1000 or 1-800-258-0330
Open year-round

Lodging: Hotel—175 rooms with phone, private bath; most rooms connect to form suites. Lodge at Bretton Woods—50 rooms with phone, TV, private bath. 200 townhouses of 2–5 bedrooms with kitchen, living room, phone, TV. Bretton Arms Inn—34 luxury rooms and suites.

Rates: Hotel—$85–$180 per person, double occupancy; $320–$350 per night for family of 4 in 2-bedroom, 1–bath family suite; children ages 6–12 in double room with parents, $25 per night; 13–17, $35; all MAP. Lodge at Bretton Woods—$98 per room per night, double occupancy; children 17 and under stay free, EP. Condominiums—$140–$220 per night per unit midweek; $185–$265 weekends and holidays, EP. Bretton Arms Inn—$130–$150 per night, double occupancy; children 6 and up, $15 per night in double room; ages 5 and under stay free, EP. Rates lower in winter.

Facilities: Indoor and outdoor pools; 18-hole golf course; putting green; golf and tennis pro shops; 12 clay tennis courts; stables; sauna; bicycle rentals; arcade of shops; ballroom; nightclub; lunch cafe; fly fishing; jogging trails; masseuse; 20 downhill ski slopes at Bretton Woods Ski Area; 100 km cross-country ski trails; game room with pinball, video games, pool, table tennis.

Family amenities: Daily children's program for ages 5–12; playground; babysitting available with advance notice.

As you emerge from Crawford Notch, high in the White Mountains, the Mount Washington Hotel looms in the distance, across an impossibly broad close-cropped lawn, like some vision from another time. Its vast white bulk framed against the Presidential Range, it looks every inch the grand resort it once was, a place where millionaires, diplomats, and potentates flocked to take the mountain air from its deep, columned porches.

Though in need of physical renovation, and buffeted by the recent disarray in New England's banking and real estate circles, the Mount Washington carries on as graciously as ever, like a proud dowager in reduced circumstances. It has become something rare and, in its way, wonderful: a sort of people's grand resort, where guests from all walks of life are treated to service once reserved only for the rich.

Even with their thin rugs and sparse furnishings, the hotel's public rooms are stately to behold. The grand lobby with its soaring ceilings and carved columns, the immense ballroom, the broad ceremonial stairways, the octagonal rotunda of the dining room—all exude a dignified, timeless grandeur.

We frankly expected our children to be overwhelmed by this huge, historic place. In fact, they loved it best of all. They regarded it as a friendly castle where they could run around and explore without fear of trespassing on things too refined or formal for children.

And what a place for exploring it is! The recreational facilities and programs at the Mount Washington are so extensive that it takes several days just to grasp what's available, let alone take advantage of it.

The focus of recreation is the hotel's "backyard," several thousand acres of woods and fields at the base of the big mountain. Clustered near the building are a large tiled outdoor pool, a croquet court, and a putting green. The pool is $3\frac{1}{2}$ feet deep at the shallow end, a bit deep for preschoolers, and there is no wading pool. A few

Photo by Nancy P. Metcalf

The rear portico and lunch terrace.

steps down the hill from the pool is a playground with a big wood climber-swingset and a sandbox.

The 12 well-maintained red clay tennis courts are also nearby; a resident pro makes matches and offers lessons, clinics, and tournaments, some of which are geared for junior players. Court time is free to guests. Beyond the tennis courts are a stocked trout river and a lovely 18-hole Donald Ross golf course. A smaller 9-hole course on the front side of the hotel is under construction.

Just inside, on the ground floor of the hotel, is a big indoor pool, a well-equipped game room, and a shopping arcade that includes a gifts and sundries shop, a clothing store, a photo studio, a florist, and a Ben & Jerry's.

Spread out at a greater distance from the main hotel are a grand Victorian-era riding stable (offering trail rides for adults and older children and guided pony rides for younger ones) and a mapped network of jogging-hiking trails. Many guests come to the Mount Washington specifically to hike the surrounding mountains; the Appalachian Mountain Club maintains a trail headquarters nearby at Crawford Notch, and the resort itself runs guided hikes of varying degrees of strenuousness.

In fact, the resort runs a very full schedule of activities of all kinds for children and adults. A typical day's offering might include aerobics classes, a golf demonstration, a feature movie, a tour of the hotel, a tennis clinic, a hike to a nearby waterfall, and a floor show by the Fred Petra Band, an excellent old-time dance and standards ensemble that's become a summer fixture at the resort. You'd be hard-pressed to come up with a song request not included in the band's 4-inch-thick stack of charts.

Many of the activities are quite suitable for children. If, however, you prefer an adults-only hike, fishing trip, or round of golf, you may enroll your children in a daily supervised program. From 9 A.M. to 4 P.M. (with an hour and a half break so the kids can lunch with their parents), the children's director shepherds the kids to tennis lessons, picnics, hikes, swims, arts and crafts, field games, and excursions to nearby children's attractions such as Santa's Village or Storyland. All this comes at no charge to resort guests with the exception of admission fees for the field trip destinations. The hotel also runs a supervised children's dinner table from 6 to 7 P.M. in a small room adjoining the main dining room.

We would, however, strongly urge you to include your kids in the regular dinner in the immense main dining room. It is an experience they won't soon forget. The room itself is a spectacle: an octagonal expanse with windows the size of garage doors looking out on the mountains. It still contains the original massive gaslight chandeliers, now electrified but still beautiful. The children get to order from their own elegantly printed menus (featuring the familiar hamburgers, grilled cheese, and chicken nuggets); the liveried waiters treat the kids like they're visiting pashas. For adults there is competently executed Continental fare, including at least one low-calorie "spa" selection every night.

Most nights, while guests linger over dessert and coffee, there's a floor show. Petra's band might appear, or a singer or comedian, or the Brettonians, the hotel's own all-employee singing group. It's a charming mixture of corn, good manners, and open-heartedness. Grandmothers take to the dance floor with their 8-year-old grandsons; sisters dance with brothers; Petra plays an unannounced medley of tunes from *Sesame Street* and *Mister Rodgers,* grinning delightedly as, one by one, the kids in the room tumble to what's going on. Everyone leaves the table full and happy.

With luck you might glimpse the raccoon family that has taken up residence in some long-forgotten crawl space behind the walls of the high cupola. To reach their outside foraging grounds, they must walk along a narrow ledge that runs around the base of the cupola, perhaps 15 feet above the heads of the guests dining below. The waiters told us that the creatures have never lost their footing and that the hotel has no intention of trying to evict them. That, we think, says something about the welcoming spirit of the place.

That spirit goes a long way toward making up for the semidilapidated state of the 175 rooms in use at the hotel (whole wings of the place are filled with tiny servants' quarters without private baths that are considered unusable today). Many of the small bathrooms contain original (circa 1903) fixtures that show every bit of their age. Water runs cold, then hot, and threatens to disappear altogether for seconds on end, making every shower an adventure. The rugs are thin, the lamps old and askew, the furniture battered white "antique" 1950s French Provincial. For years various owners and managers have promised that renovation is imminent, but so far the cost has remained out of reach for any of them. In the meantime, however, the rooms still have their door-sized windows, their 14-foot ceilings, and their glorious views. They're clean, the mattresses are comfortable, and your children, in any event, will probably be oblivious to any of this.

Another advantage to the nonrenovated condition is that it somehow brings guests closer to the history of the place. This was the scene of the 1944 Bretton Woods U.N. Monetary Conference that shaped the monetary system of the free world, and for years it hosted important tennis tournaments. Brass nameplates mark the doors of rooms where various dignitaries once stayed; see if you can find John Maynard Keynes, Henry Morgenthau, Charles Evans Hughes, Arthur Ashe, Ken Rosewall, or Roy Emerson.

Though the most intimate experience of this place comes from staying in the hotel itself, the resort has several other more up-to-date lodging options that give you full access to all recreational facilities. They are also open in the winter, while the unheated hotel must close down, and are thus convenient for skiers taking advantage of the resort's cross-country ski facilities or the nearby Bretton Woods Ski Area.

Across Route 302 from the hotel is the Lodge at Bretton Woods, a 50-room motel with standard rooms, all with paired double beds, television, air conditioning, and mountain views. It has an indoor heated pool, a sauna, a spa, pool , and its own restaurant, Darby's. A 10-minute walk from the main hotel is the Bretton Arms, an exquisitely restored Victorian era bed and breakfast (we think this a little too elegant for the average child, however). Finally, the nearby Bretton Woods Condominiums, fully furnished one- to four-bedroom modern townhouses, usually list 70–80 units in a rental pool.

The Sagamore

Bolton Landing, NY 12814
518-644-9400 or 1-800-358-3585
Open year-round

Lodging: 100 rooms in main hotel with private bath, cable color TV, phone; some rooms can be combined into suites; 240 rooms in lodges, including 120 rooms equipped similarly to main hotel rooms and 120 suites containing private bath, kitchenette, living room with queen-size sofa beds, separate bedroom, color cable TV, fireplace, terrace or balcony. Lodge suites can connect to a second bedroom.

Rates: $120–$222 per person per day, double occupancy, MAP. For children sharing room or suite, ages 2 and under, no charge; 3–12, $24; 13-17, $50 per day MAP. Family packages, MAP in lodges only, including children's program for ages 3-12: 2 days, 2 nights for 2 adults plus 1 child, $562–$701; plus 2 children, $614–$754; plus 3 children, $666–$806; extra night, 2 adults plus 1 child, $272–$342; plus 2 children, $300–$370; plus 3 children, $328–$398. Golf packages also available. Rates lower before May and after October.

Facilities: Lake swimming beach; motorboat and bicycle rentals; parasailing; indoor pool; spa with sauna, steam room, whirlpool, massage, facials, exercise equipment and instruction; lake excursion and dinner boat; 2 formal dining rooms; café; lunch terrace; lunch and dinner grill room in golf clubhouse; nightclub; 18-hole golf course; putting green; croquet; 2 Har-Tru, 2 all-weather outdoor tennis courts; 2 indoor tennis courts; tennis and golf instruction, pro shops;

racquetball court; gift shop; art gallery; walking-jogging trail; game room with pool, Nintendo, video games, table tennis; volleyball; basketball; board games; surrey rides. Winter— cross-country trails at golf course; cross-country ski rentals and instruction; shuttle buses to Gore Mountain ski area; skating rinks at golf course and at main hotel.

Family amenities: Supervised all-day programs for ages 3–5 and 6–13; supervised children's dinner table; outdoor playground; babysitting available with advance notice.

Around Lake George any mention of the Sagamore elicits raised eyebrows and admiring sighs followed by exclamations on how expensive it is. The locals have got it right. This stylishly restored and expanded grand lakefront resort has all the elements in place: comfortable, impeccably maintained rooms; lavish recreational facilities; dazzling public rooms and grounds; responsive and intelligent service; quantities of excellent food. Oh, and one of the most well-organized, well-supplied, and thoughtfully designed children's programs we have ever encountered. Of course, a three-day stay will set back a family of four a cool $1,200 (on the "economical" family plan and before tennis or golf fees or taxes). But in this case, you truly do get what you pay for.

There's been a grand resort hotel on Green Island in Lake George, across a short bridge from the bustling tourist hamlet of Bolton Landing, for more than 100 years. Fires ruined the first two hotels; the current main hotel building went up in stages in the 1920s and 1930s. It closed in 1981 after its then-owners refused (in spite of history) to install a sprinkler system. At that point, a wealthy local family bought the place. Two years and millions of dollars later, after endless regulatory and environmental struggles, the Sagamore reopened in its present incarnation. In addition to the gloriously renovated white clapboard main building (which finally got its sprinklers), the resort now includes the separate "lodge" buildings, lakefront structures of the stained-wood-and-glass variety. These have privately owned vacation condominiums on their top floors while the bottom two floors contain hotel rooms and suites.

Although families can stay anywhere, the suites offer by far the most hospitable accommodations. For starts, they have small kitchens equipped with just enough utensils to prepare a lunch or snack and small round dining tables to eat them at. Their high-ceilinged, fireplaced living rooms have ultra-cushiony sectional sofas (which open into queen-size beds if desired), sturdy, modern versions of Adirondack twig furniture, quilts and wall hangings that reinforce the chic-woodsy feeling, and balconies or terraces looking out onto the lake (environmental regulations severely limited the amount of lakefront vegetation that could be removed so the views are partially blocked by trees and brush). The suites come with at least one bedroom, containing either a king-size bed or two double beds; they can also be connected to the hotel room on the same floor. Because each floor contains only one suite and one single room, sound transmission is kept to a minimum.

The lodges are separate from the main hotel, but the island is small enough that the walk is not a problem. And they're serviced as attentively as rooms in the main hotel. Every night on your return from dinner you'll find your beds turned down, with chocolates on the pillow and the next day's schedule of activities on the bedside table (the schedule even gives the weather forecast).

The children's program is itself housed in one of the lodges in a converted condominium unit near the sturdy outdoor playscape and basketball court (in a characteristic touch, the backboard can be raised or lowered according to the size of the players). The program operates weekends from Memorial Day weekend until late June and daily thereafter through the Labor Day weekend.

The program is split into two age groups—one for children ages 3–kindergarten, the other for children who've completed kindergarten and older. Both are staffed by summering schoolteachers or college students. The headquarters suite is well-stocked with games, toys, art supplies, and videos for rainy days.

The younger children stick close to the condo where they fill their days with nature walks, sand play, story hours, kite flying, wading pools, and face-painting. Older children have similar activities

The main hotel.

keyed to their age levels and also visit the Sagamore's large new indoor swimming pool every morning. The program runs 9 A.M. to 4 P.M. every day and includes a box lunch. The schedule is planned thoughtfully and well in advance; this is clearly much more than a babysitting service.

If you like, you can also drop the kids off for a supervised dinner-playtime that runs nightly 6 to 9 P.M. The kids wolf down a meal at Mister Brown's, the most informal of the hotel's eating places, with a menu that runs heavily to burgers and deli sandwiches. Then they adjourn to the playground to burn off all the calories they've just consumed. Meanwhile, you can dine in peace and splendor either on well-cooked Continental cuisine in the main dining room or on pricey French food in the Trillium (for a hefty surcharge to the basic MAP rate). Both dining rooms overlook the beautiful lake.

A drawback of the children's program, however, is that it doesn't take kids under the age of 3. At dinner in the main dining room, we saw lots of parents neglect their smoked trout and beef bourgignon while tending to squirming, fussy infants and toddlers. The dining room staff seemed to have a plentiful supply of high chairs and booster seats and betrayed not a hint of impatience with the bedlam, but, still, the parents were missing the serene dining experience they were presumably paying for.

By contrast, breakfast with the children in the dining room is downright fun. It's served buffet style, our favorite, because it minimizes the wait time with ravenous little people. Here you can even watch a puff-hatted chef cook your fried eggs or omelets to order. There is a separate good-for-you spread with yogurt, herbal tea, fruits, and whole-grain cereals. But our favorite touch is the children's buffet table, the only one we've ever seen. It's as elegantly furnished and arranged as the regular table, but stands about a foot and a half high and is stocked with guaranteed kid-pleasers: Frosted Flakes in single-serving boxes, French toast precut into bite-sized pieces, chocolate milk, and a stack of Sagamore coloring books (complete with Crayola four-packs).

The Sagamore offers the sort of plush, all-encompassing recreational facilities you'd expect of a place this luxurious. The most recent renovation included a total restoration of the 1928 Donald Ross golf course, which contains a beautiful stone-and-wood clubhouse-restaurant that's worth a visit even if you don't golf. The course is on the mainland, perhaps a 10-minute ride from the hotel; the resort runs a shuttle van for guests who don't want to take their own cars.

The tennis center, with four outdoor and two indoor courts, offers matchmaking, clinics, and tournaments. Twice a week in the summer, there are special clinics for children ages 11–16. Tennis is on the island proper, a few steps from the lodges. Both golf and tennis cost extra.

Surprisingly, there's no outdoor pool at the Sagamore. There is, however, Lake George, a clean, refreshing body of water in spite of its size and the intensity of development on some (though by no means all) of its shore frontage. The lake beach here is ingeniously designed as a sort of natural swimming pool. It's completely enclosed (except for a narrow outlet at the deeper end) by a wood deck and underwater fencing, which smooth out the rough waves that develop so easily on the big lake. The shallow end, approached via wood steps covered with slime-proof, slip-proof carpeting, is a bit under 3 feet deep. The bottom, sandy with a few scattered stones, reaches perhaps $5\frac{1}{2}$ feet at its deepest point. There is no sloping beach; a wood seawall goes straight down from the water's edge. Behind this the resort has trucked in lovely white sand, perfect for castle-building. However, nonswimming children shorter than about 40 inches really have no comfortable access to the water; the ones we saw had to be carried in and held by their parents.

While very young children may find slim pickings here, the opposite is true for preadolescents and teenagers. The game room (in the same building as the indoor tennis courts) contains pinball, video games, pool, and even Nintendo. The rooms themselves have cable color television and HBO so no teenager need go unplugged-in. For a steepish fee the resort will happily rent out motorboats fully capable of pulling water skiers. Also for rent are mountain bikes (helmets commendably included) for exploring the surrounding countryside.

With the kids happily tucked away in the children's programs, parents are free to enjoy not only the sports facilities, but the Sagamore's fancy adults-only amenities. The spa—with elegant his-and-hers locker rooms—runs a full schedule of exercise classes every day. You can have your pores cleaned out with a facial and a steambath, your aches soothed with a full-body massage, and your dead skin flaked away with a loofah treatment.

For a romantic night out (included in the MAP), try a dinner cruise on the *Morgan*. This excursion boat looks like a burnished wood antique, but in fact is only 4 years old, with up-to-the-minute mechanical parts and safety features. Fitted neatly into the kids' dinner time frame, the $2\frac{1}{2}$-hour cruise begins with a cocktail hour on the top deck, followed by a formal meal of Cornish game hen served below, on white linen, with silver and crystal, a plush carpet underfoot and recorded classical guitar music playing softly in the background. You'll be taken to the nether reaches of the lake, past some lovely old Adirondack camps, primeval granite-and-pine shorelines and islands which, on closer view, prove to be well-populated with intrepid families camping in tents and lean-tos—the polar opposite, you instantly realize, of your Sagamore experience.

Samoset Resort

Rockport, ME 04856
207-594-2511 or 1-800-341-1650
Open year-round

Lodging: 150 rooms and suites in main hotel with private bath, air conditioning, color cable TV, some with refrigerator; 72 condominium units with air conditioning, color cable TV, kitchenette, living-dining room, balcony or patio.

Rates: Summer—EP hotel rooms $150–$230 per night; time-share condominiums, 1 bedroom $260, 2 bedrooms $300 per night; MAP $130 per person, double occupancy, hotel only; AP $139 per person, double occupancy, hotel only. Rates lower in fall, spring, winter. Special packages available for holiday weekends, school vacation weeks, golf holidays, etc. No charge for children under 16 staying in same room with parents, EP only.

Facilities: 18-hole oceanside golf course, putting green, practice trap, and driving range; 1 indoor, 2 lighted outdoor tennis courts; indoor and outdoor swimming pools; indoor and outdoor heated whirlpool baths; walking, jogging, and fitness trails; 2 racquetball courts; Nautilus and Universal equipment; exercise classes; cycling and rowing machines; massage therapists; tanning room; croquet course; shuffleboard; badminton; volleyball; bicycle rentals; basketball; charter boat cruises; pro golf, tennis, and gift shops. Winter—10 km groomed cross-country ski trails; ice-skating rink.

Family amenities: Supervised children's activities daily in

summer, on weekends, and for school vacation holidays in winter; swingsets; video arcade.

The map says Maine on it, and the view out to sea certainly looks Down East enough, but in every other way Samoset Resort could just as well be 3,000 miles away on the California coast. It bills itself as the "Pebble Beach of the East," a claim we consider pretty accurate.

This is a modern luxury resort which caters to affluent golfers and other pleasure-seekers. Completed in 1974 to replace a fire-gutted shuttered Victorian-era grand hotel, the Samoset spreads sleekly across its spectacular 230-acre oceanfront site. This resort looks and acts contemporary, with its angular buildings and loving concern for the easy passage and parking of its guests' automobiles.

In the summer golf is king at the Samoset. The course, renowned in golfing circles, almost completely encircles the hotel. It is literally not possible to walk from the hotel to the water's edge on resort property if you are not playing a round of golf. Instead, you must walk the long way around, to a public access road off the grounds, to reach the ocean.

But for a family that includes a golf-loving parent or two, Samoset may well be the next best thing to heaven. While the parents attempt the challenging course, the resort's lively young recreational staffers will run the children a merry round of games, swims, and arts and crafts in a supervised program that starts each day at 9 A.M., continues through lunch, and finishes up at 2 P.M. One hot, sunny day during our stay, we found our kids deliriously dashing between the outdoor whirlpool and the swimming pool, having just polished off a BLT and an ice-cream bar for lunch.

Families have a choice of accommodations here. The hotel proper includes many suites and connecting rooms suitable for families with children. The suites feature a living room with a sofabed, a refrigerator, and a separate bedroom. The connecting rooms are somewhat less costly ("costly" being a relative term at this high-priced resort), but lack refrigerators or living rooms. Guests at the hotel can opt for the Modified American Plan rate, which includes breakfast and dinner in any of the hotel's several eating places (more about them later). There are also good deals to be had in package plans.

Families willing to fend for themselves at mealtimes can save a lot of money by staying in one of the Samoset's rental time-share condominiums located a very short walk from the main hotel. Every one has a balcony or terrace and an ocean view, as well as a living area and kitchenette. There's a coin laundry in every building. Groceries are readily available from a large supermarket in a shopping plaza just outside the resort's entrance road. Both the hotel and the time-share units contain plush, modern furnishings and decor.

In spite of its focus on golf, Samoset has not neglected its other recreational facilities. The outdoor pool, surrounded by a broad and many-leveled wood deck, is large and heated to the proper refreshing temperature. Guests looking for utter relaxation could easily spend the entire day here, dozing in the comfortable lounge chairs, dipping into the whirlpool, and strolling over to the poolside

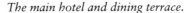

The main hotel and dining terrace.

Photo by Nancy P. Metcalf

snack bar for a simple sandwich lunch. There is no children's wading pool. The shallow end of the big pool is about 3 feet deep.

Surrounding the pool are other nongolf amenities, including a couple of big, sturdy wood swingsets, basketball and volleyball courts, and two outdoor tennis courts, all of which are free to Samoset guests.

This year-round resort also includes an up-to-date fitness center. You can play a round of tennis on the indoor court, sweat off your meals on the racquetball court or on a weight or rowing machine, get your stresses pounded out with a massage, jump around in an aerobics class, or take a dip in the indoor pool or whirlpool. According to the resort's management, many families make use of the indoor sports facilities in the dead of winter, when Samoset offers a temptingly priced school vacation family package that includes organized children's activities. Outdoors in the winter, Samoset turns its golf course into a marked and groomed 10-km cross-country ski course. All these activities cost extra.

Meals at the Samoset can be taken in one of two main dining rooms. The more formal, called Marcel's, is a pastel-hued, hushed space looking out to sea. A standard children's menu thoughtfully complements the very sophisticated adult bill of fare, but be forewarned, the stately pace of service may tax the sitting-still abilities of your youngsters. Breakfast, also served here, comes faster and features the standard—by which we mean immense—menu typical of luxury resorts.

The second dining room, the Breakwater Lounge, is open for lunch, snacks, and light dinners such as pizza, nachos, and burgers, served with considerably more dispatch. In good weather the same menu is served on the Breakwater Patio just outside. Both overlook the water.

No matter where you eat you may find yourselves mesmerized by the sea view. One night we looked up from our dinners to behold a perfect rainbow making a complete arc across the horizon. Afterward, we went outside and played a round of croquet on the permanent, putting-green-quality course. We felt like Alice in Wonderland.

Venturesome older children might enjoy a walk out the mile-long stone pier that juts into Penobscot Bay at Samoset's southern border. As we mentioned before, you'll have to walk off the resort grounds and around to get there (and when you do, you'll have a splendid view back to Samoset itself). The pier is made of immense granite blocks fitted more or less together. Watch your small ones closely, however. It's possible to fall into a crack between two blocks and plunge four or five feet down. Also, don't even attempt this adventure with a stroller. Be sure to stop along the way to watch the lobstermen checking their pots, or the locals fishing. You can fish, too. The concierge has poles for rent, and the kitchen will clean and cook your catch.

Midway out the pier is Samoset's boat dock. Here you can catch a chartered schooner or a deep-sea fishing boat; the resort can arrange both on request (at a price, of course). Other resort outings that might appeal to older children include time on a boat with a Maine lobsterman or a sea kayak trip.

Samoset's midcoast Maine location gives guests easy access to the famous delights of this part of the world. Quaint and tasteful Camden is a short drive down the coast. Ferries to Matinicus and Vinalhaven islands leave from Rockland, just below Camden—if, that is, you can tear yourself away from the golf course.

Skytop Lodge

Skytop, PA 18357
717-595-7401 or 1-800-345-7SKY (1-800-345-7759)
Open year-round

Lodging: 285 rooms in main lodge and 8 cottages, all with TV, private bath, telephone; cottages have washer-dryer unit.

Rates: $249 per night for 2 adults in room with king- or queen-size bed, AP. Up to 2 children under 18 stay free in same room with parents for service charge of $10 per night per child; 10 percent discount from adult rate for children occupying separate rooms. Rates slightly higher on weekends, lower November through April.

Facilities: Indoor and outdoor pools; children's indoor pool; whirlpool; 18-hole golf course; 5 Har-Tru and 2 all-weather tennis courts; paddle tennis court; archery range; lawn bowling court; croquet; bicycles for rent; private stocked trout stream; private stocked lake; lake swimming beach; rowboats and canoes; card rooms; marked hiking, nature, and exercise trails; covered, open-sided sports pavilion with volleyball, shuffleboard, and miniature golf in summer, artificial ice-skating rink in winter; archery range; groomed cross-country ski trails; health club with exercise room, whirlpool, and sauna; small alpine ski slope with 2 Poma lifts; tea room with snack bar, sundries, VCR, and tape rentals; game room with video arcade, billiards, table tennis.

Family amenities: Playground; summer day camp for children ages 3–12; special family weekends; babysitting available with advance notice.

Our visit to Skytop began with a discouraging drive through the
Poconos, past what seemed like dozens of tacky honeymoon
palaces. With each new sign advertising heart-shaped bathtubs we
became increasingly worried about what we were getting ourselves
into. Then, at the crest of the hill, we spotted a group of deer
peacefully grazing at the edge of an immaculate, beautiful golf
course. A few seconds later, an enormous grand stone building came
into view at the end of a vast sloping green lawn. It looked like some
sort of English manor transplanted to Pennsylvania. It was, of
course, Skytop Lodge.

Built in 1928 as a private club, Skytop lives on today as a
luxurious, quietly elegant, and skillfully run full-service grand
resort. A recent $2 million renovation has left it with modern, richly
comfortable guest rooms and refurbished wood-paneled public
rooms.

Within its 5,500 acres of meadows, mountains, lakes, and streams,
Skytop provides virtually every recreation imaginable that does not
require salt water. You can golf, play tennis, swim, fish, hike, ski,
even go lawn bowling or try your hand at archery. Or, if you like,
you can spend the entire day in a rocking chair on Skytop's long
south porch, admiring the impeccably manicured formal gardens
and the distant views of the Delaware Water Gap beyond. Three
times a day (and dressed up at dinner), you will venture into
Skytop's high-ceilinged formal dining room for a perfectly served
meal, which is included in your American Plan rate.

Now for the amazing part: this will not necessarily bankrupt you.
For the past few years Skytop has permitted children under 18 to
stay free in the same room with their parents. This includes 14-year-
olds with refrigerator-clearing appetites as well as 4-year-olds. Of
course, some modest conditions apply (a $10-per-child-per-night
addition to your service charge, and no more than two children per
room). Still, it means a family can spend a week at this utterly
luxurious place for a base rate of under $2,000.

The same-room-with-parents requirement isn't all that onerous,
either, given the caliber of rooms at Skytop. Families with children
should opt for one of the cottages, whose rooms are somewhat
larger than those in the main lodge. Located a short walk from the
main building, they're actually misnamed, being simply satellite

Photo courtesy of Skytop Lodge

The main hotel and formal gardens.

mini-hotels containing four rooms each. The rooms can be hooked up into suites or taken separately. The rooms are large, with small outdoor terraces, and some contain a fold-out sofabed in addition to a queen-size master bed. Each cottage also has an alcove at the end of its entry hall with a washing machine and dryer, free for the use of guests and a blessing for parents with untidy children.

The rate structure is just one of the things Skytop is doing to attract families with children. The other principal one is Camp-in-the-Clouds, the day camp it opens during the summer season. Overseen by a day care professional and staffed by college students, it operates out of a clubhouse next to one of the resort's two lakes. Children arrive after breakfast. Mornings are devoted to crafts, games, boating (with lifejackets on and a counselor aboard, of course), golf and tennis lessons, hikes, croquet, and the like. Children return to their parents for lunch from noon to 2 P.M. Weather permitting, the children are taken swimming in the afternoon at Skytop's lifeguarded lake bathing beach. An L-shaped dock partially encloses a shallow swimming area. On the other side the lake deepens abruptly; older children can dive here.

In non-day-camp hours, Skytop's swimming pool complex is a magnet to children. There's an outdoor pool with a 3-foot-deep shallow end. Right next to this is the glass-walled, skylit indoor pool complex, which includes an adult-size pool, a children's wading pool, and a whirlpool. Swimmers can move freely between the indoor and outdoor areas.

Off-season, Skytop arranges a series of special family weekends. January "all sports" weekends feature cold-weather exertions including sleighrides and toboggan runs. Early spring brings a series of "country weekends" featuring squaredances, hayrides, target shoots, and on occasion farm animals in the elegant lobby.

Older children might enjoy Skytop's enormous basement game room, with video, billiards, and table tennis. They can also join adults in some of the scheduled activities. Every morning, for instance, the resort's full-time naturalist leads a hike to some natural point of interest. There are putting tournaments, junior tennis clinics, and the like.

Meanwhile adults have a choice of all the facilities already mentioned, plus the carefully maintained golf and tennis complexes. Sports are done correctly here; you must, for instance, wear proper golf and tennis clothing to be permitted to play. The tennis and golf pros offer private lessons and matchmaking services.

There is, however, nary a heart-shaped bathtub in the place.

Saltwater Retreats

The Chalfonte

301 Howard Street
Cape May, NJ 08204
609-884-8409
Open Memorial Day through early October

Lodging: 104 rooms in main hotel and 2 neighboring cottages, 11 with private bath, the rest with shared bath. Franklin Street Cottage, a separate 4-bedroom, 8-person cottage with sitting room, bath, refrigerator, rented as a single unit.

Rates: Main hotel and cottages, $108–$135 per day double occupancy, MAP; Franklin Street Cottage, $175 per day plus MAP meal charges. Children under 15 stay free in same room with parents but pay MAP meal charges: adults, $25 per day; ages infant–1, $3; 2–6, $6; 7–10, $11; 11–14, $15. Discounts for midweek, week-long, and month-long stays.

Facilities: Workshops and other scheduled events; bar with nightly entertainment.

Family amenities: Supervised children's dining room; children's theater workshop; afternoon supervised program when demand warrants.

Don't look for too many signs of the twentieth century at the Chalfonte, Cape May's oldest surviving hotel. Since 1876 sea breezes have cooled the rooms, not air conditioning, and there are no TVs, radios, or telephones—and few private baths—to evoke the modern world. Instead, Victorian charm and grace prevail in this wood relic of classic seaside architecture, with its two-story porches that creak and sag from a century of salt air, its striped awnings, and gingerbread accents on post and pillar.

Indeed the Chalfonte seems the very essence of Cape May, an ingratiating tip of land evoking New England Victoriana more than any other vacation spot in the state of New Jersey. This national landmark community bills itself the "Nation's Oldest Seaside Resort," and its private houses and many bed & breakfasts are typically restored gems of gabled design and quaint coloration, interspersed with small specialty shops.

The Chalfonte stands central to all this like a maiden aunt who's seen it all and still keeps a fond watch. For breakfast and dinner every day she opens her doors to all who can't get enough of the superb Southern home cooking faithfully prepared (and nationally hailed) for decades by Helen Dickerson and her daughters, Dot and Lucille.

Only hotel guests are assured of daily seatings in the great rectangular dining room, which has a semiformal air of oceanliner clubbiness. Men must wear jackets at dinner, though it's no affront to drape them on chair backs on hot nights. Guests are seated in thoughtfully mixed groups, and conversation is egged on effortlessly by the remarkable cuisine. During our stay we shared a table with a delightful pair of hotel regulars, elderly widows who regaled us with Chalfonte anecdotes and Cape May gossip that ranged from generations past right up to the present.

Such delicious adult conversation is made possible by the fact that children ages 6 and under are served in a well-supervised dining room of their own set just off the main room. Kids enjoy the same cuisine (with whatever improvisations are necessary for their peculiar appetites) and are kept amused with playground and group activity until their parents are finished with their own meals.

Apart from its gingerbread architecture, food is the Chalfonte's main, justly renowned, attraction. Meals frame the day's activities with rich, delicious variety. Breakfast is a cardiologist's nightmare: eggs perfectly cooked in bacon fat, meltaway homemade biscuits, fried weakfish filets and—no exaggeration—the best sausage links

Photo courtesy of The Chalfonte

The main hotel.

we have ever had. There are also soup bowls of Helen Dickerson's addictive spoon bread, a baked batter of cornmeal, eggs, shortening, and milk, crispy on top and puddinglike at heart. Dinners are equally distinctive, with such Dickersonian delights as eggplant casserole, broiled bluefish, truly memorable crabfish cakes, savory roast meats, fried chicken to write home about, and flake-crusted pies.

Chalfonte rooms are typically spartan, but clean and well tended, with a washbasin and comfortable mattresses. You can still twiddle the disconnected wall gaslight fixtures. Renovations and repairs are almost constantly in progress, and several off-season work weekends offer guests free room and board in exchange for elbow grease. Bathrooms down the hall are adequately outfitted and maintained.

Families most often stay in any of three cottages on the hotel grounds. Our lodging, in the Sewell Street cottage, was a two-room second-floor suite with a double bed in one room and twin beds for the kids in the other. Each was cooled quite adequately by the salt air wafting through the screens.

The Chalfonte doesn't have athletic amenities like tennis, golf, or swimming pools. The hotel programs instead cater to guests' spirits, with Gilbert and Sullivan weekends, candlelight concerts, classic Hollywood films, and quality painting and photography workshops.

For children ages 6–12 the Chalfonte arranges several week-long performance workshops. In the morning and late afternoon the kids practice mime and storytelling, with a midday break for lunch and the beach. The resort also offers limited daytime child care for preschoolers as demand warrants.

Beyond the Chalfonte Cape May offers the typical patchwork of seaside honky-tonk. The beach and a tiny boardwalk are barely two blocks from the hotel, and along the way are miniature golf courses, coffee shops, and many good restaurants and delis. All this can be enjoyed the old-fashioned way, with no car. The beach is wide, popular, and one of the Jersey shore's consistently cleanest. It was virtually untouched by the infamous pollution crisis of a few summers back. Taffy, fudge, and souvenir shops sweeten and enliven the pier, and on rainy days the beachfront movie house will strike up unscheduled family film matinees (we wandered happily into one such showing of *Honey, I Shrunk the Kids*).

Other attractions, a bit farther away, though still in walking distance, include daily fishing cruises, sailboat rentals, a worthwhile tour of the 1859 Cape May Lighthouse, and any number of Victorian house tours. Cape May makes for a great long weekend or short week of summering, and the Chalfonte is as quintessential a place as any from which to enjoy its innocent charms.

Chatham Bars Inn

Shore Road
Chatham, MA 02633
508-945-0096 or 1-800-527-4884
Open year-round

Lodging: 44 rooms in main inn; 108 rooms in 26 lodges and cottages of 1–8 bedrooms; many rooms in main inn and large cottages form connecting suites; all with private bath, phone, cable television; many with small refrigerator, terrace, or balcony.

Rates: Double or twin bedrooms in main inn and cottages, $25–$350 per day for 2 persons; family suites in main inn, $405 per day for 3 persons, $460 per day for 4; bedroom-living room cottage suite, $375 per day for 2 persons; 2-bedroom-living room cottage suite, $590–$700 per day for 4 persons; rates for cottages vary according to number in party, ages of children, and size of cottage. All MAP. Rates lower in June and September, lowest before and after those months.

Facilities: Ocean beach; heated freshwater pool; 5 all-weather tennis courts; croquet; shuffleboard; badminton; horseshoes; sport fishing charters; putting green; 9-hole town golf course adjacent to inn.

Family amenities: Supervised summer recreation program for children ages 4 and up 9:30 A.M.–noon and 2–4:30 P.M. Children's supper and evening entertainment, 6–9 P.M. Babysitting available with advance notice.

Located at the elbow of Cape Cod facing the open Atlantic, Chatham is a postcard of a resort town. And in the midst of the town's grandest neighborhood, down the shore road from Georgian hydrangea-wreathed waterfront mansions, sits the Chatham Bars Inn, the very picture of an elegant beachfront resort.

The World War I-vintage main inn was expensively renovated in the mid-1980s and the 26 shingled "cottages" on the property (some are more like small inns in themselves) are in the process of being upgraded to the same exacting standards. In its present incarnation, the inn caters to moneyed, tasteful guests in search of a soothing, private oceanside stay—children included.

As hushed and private as it is, the inn is nonetheless located near some of the best the Cape has to offer. The wild dunes and surf of the Cape Cod National Seashore lie just a few minutes' drive to the north, and a 5-minute walk brings you to Chatham's business district. (Don't even think of taking your car; the town's charming shops and restaurants draw hordes of tourists in the summer months and parking is impossible.)

The inn's main building perches on a hill overlooking Pleasant Bay, a long piece of saltwater sheltered from the Atlantic by a barrier sandbar stretching south from the National Seashore (although accessible only by water or by four-wheel-drive vehicle, the sandbar is actually the very southern tip of the seashore). Many of the resort's cottages are directly on the waterfront, with brilliant and unobstructed views of the bay, the sandbar, and the ocean beyond. This is a working bay, filled with pleasure craft and commercial fishing boats, so there's always something interesting to see.

The resort offers several room configurations suitable for families. Some of the smaller cottages can be rented whole, and three have kitchenettes. Several of the larger cottages can split into two- or four-room suites. The main inn also has connecting suites. One caveat: some of the upper-floor rooms both in the cottages and in the main inn have balcony rails that children could slip through or easily climb over. The cottages behind the inn do not have ocean views, but they are within easy walking distance of the dining room and beach. Most of the shore cottages are so far from the inn you'll need to drive to meals and activities, but these cottages have spectacular views. Also, to get to the inn from even the closest shorefront cottages, you have to cross a public road. This is, in short, no place to let very young children walk unsupervised. All the rooms are tastefully, even luxuriously furnished in sturdy Queen Anne-style furniture.

The resort's activities center, naturally enough, is on the beach compound down the hill and across the shore road from the main building. There's a large expanse of sand for castle-building, wading, and sunbathing, though most swimmers seem to prefer the heated beachfront pool. Its shallow end, however, is too deep for average-sized preschoolers and there is no wading pool. Near the beach and pool is a bathhouse with showers and changing rooms as well as an endless supply of big, fluffy beach towels. And behind the beach is a breezy grill room that serves fat sandwiches, hamburgers, and cold salads for lunch.

Down the beach from the swimming area are the resort's five tennis courts, where a resident pro offers instruction and matchmaking services.

And from the beach you can catch the resort launch for the 5-minute ride to the outer bar—the beach on the barrier sandbar on

The main inn.

Photo courtesy of Chatham Bars Inn

the other side of the bay. The ocean side of the outer bar features thundering surf—too thundering, in our view, for all but older children skilled at ocean swimming. We far preferred the bay side of the outer bar, where shifting tides and currents create clear, shallow, calm tidal pools that warm rapidly in the summer sun and serve as safe natural wading areas. The resort will pack a lunch if you want to picnic here.

The beach compound is also the center of the resort's extensive daytime children's program. Children ages 4 1/2 or above gather every morning in a room attached to the bathhouse (with a great water view). In nice weather they'll go for a nature walk, fly kites, or go wading. The playroom's stock of games and art supplies diverts them on rainy days. The program breaks for lunch and resumes again in the afternoon. It is included in the room fee.

Just before dinner you can bring your children back to the playhouse for the evening program. They'll be served a dinner of burgers or hot dogs in the beachfront grill, followed by a make-your-own-sundae party, lawn games, or perhaps a visit from a local magician. In the meantime you can enjoy a leisurely adult meal in the resort's elegant main dining room. We heartily recommend this option, unless your 6-year-old actually likes sitting still at a formal table for an hour and a half while savoring asparagus soup, escargots, watercress-strawberry salad, poached salmon, and Key lime pie.

On the other hand, kids enjoy the main dining room for breakfast, when waiters promptly serve up your choices from the gigantic menu of juices, fruits, cereals, eggs, omelettes, meats, fish, pastries, pancakes, and waffles.

Within an easy walk or short drive from the resort are two kid-pleasing sights. One is the Chatham fish pier, which abuts the northernmost waterfront cottages. Beginning at about 3 P.M. daily, the town's sizable fleet of fishing boats starts threading its way through the bay channel to discharge the day's catch. The pier—actually a good-sized fish warehouse attached to several piers—features a second-story observation deck. You can hang over the sturdy, high rail and watch the fishermen, clad in hip-high rubber boots, grapple thousands of fish out of the boats' holds and into the depths of the warehouse.

Another not-to-be-missed outing is the Chatham Band's regular Friday evening concert at the gingerbread bandstand in Kate Gould Park, an easy 10-minute walk from the inn's back door. In their red and blue uniforms, with brass buttons and gold braid, the mostly white-haired local musicians look like they just stepped out of 1910. Buy a balloon on the way in, and don't forget a blanket to spread on the ground. Midway through the concert, the conductor clears a space around the bandstand and invites all the children down for a promenade.

The resort also runs a schedule of general activities, many of them family-oriented. There's a weekly Wednesday night clambake and sing-along at the beach house; a weekly theme party; morning nature and fitness walks; volleyball, shuffleboard, and putting tournaments; and sand sculpture and kite-flying contests.

With all this, however, the resort seems unusually respectful of family privacy. If you choose, you will have no trouble spending a week here without feeling coerced into interacting with anyone else. If, on the other hand, you count new acquaintances as one of the joys of a summer vacation, you might be disappointed here.

No description of a Chatham-based resort would be complete without a mention of the awesome natural phenomenon that has been unfolding less than a mile from the inn's beach. During a winter storm on January 2, 1987, the ocean broke through the outer bar. It turned what had once been the southern tip of the sandbar into a skinny sand island, and exposed a big piece of Pleasant Bay to the full force of the Atlantic. Only a few yards wide at first, the breach is a half mile wide now, and still expanding. The pounding waves and surging currents have destroyed several waterfront homes and removed the beach from the fronts of several others, while carrying sand to the beaches of other waterfront properties (the Chatham Bars Inn included). The currents and shifting underwater sand drifts have made navigating this stretch of Pleasant Bay a hazardous undertaking, and swimmers would be wise to keep close to shore.

Goose Cove Lodge

Goose Cove Road
Sunset, ME 04683
207-348-2508 (summer) or 207-767-3003 (winter)
Open early June through mid-September

Lodging: 10 suites and rooms located in annexes to main lodge, 1–2 bedrooms, some with living room, fireplace. 11 cottages sleeping 2–6, all with sundeck, fireplace, refrigerator or kitchenette.

Rates: $410–$550 per person per week ($465–$625 in August), MAP. Children under 2, $120 per week; 2–4, $185 per week; 5–11, half adult rate.

Facilities: Ocean beach; marked nature trails; canoes and rowboats; recreation hall with pool, table tennis, and video library; gift shop.

Family amenities: Supervised children's dinner hour; babysitting during dinner for children under 2; toys and books available in main lodge.

You can't get much deeper into coastal Maine than this. Located down a long dirt road, at the edge of Deer Isle in East Penobscot Bay, Goose Cove Lodge is a serene, rustic, yet intellectually stimulating haven for thoughtful, sociable guests.

The property includes 70 acres of woods and rocky coastline, most of which remain primevally undisturbed. The resort's main lodge and cottages cluster on a gentle rise above a gravelly crescent beach with stunning views of pine-covered granite islands beyond.

Photo by Nancy P. Metcalf

The main lodge.

Goose Cove Lodge seems just about perfect for Maine-o-philes with portable babies and toddlers, or nature-loving older children. However, kids who demand lots of hands-on sports, heated swimming pools, and the like may get restless here.

The main lodge here is truly the center of activity. With its walls of fascinating books (guests can help themselves, and the library includes a wonderful collection of children's books), comfortable chairs, burnished wood tables and floors, and array of exquisite local arts and handcrafts, it looks very much like the living room of a pair of well-to-do college professors (of art and English literature, perhaps). But there is nothing formal here; this is the woods and guests are instantly at home.

For all its sophisticated-rustic charm, the lodge is actually relatively new and, from the outside, architecturally featureless. But George and Eleanor Pavloff, longtime owners of Goose Cove Lodge, added on a spectacular dining area on the beach side of the lodge that makes the interior truly extraordinary. It's basically a half-octagon, virtually all windows, against which the dining tables are set. The living room opens into this light-filled space.

Every night adult guests gather in the living room for bring-your-own drinks and lodge-supplied hors d'oeuvres. By the end of a week's stay, they are old and dear friends. That happens in part because of the intimacy of the place, and in part because younger children aren't around to interrupt. Instead, they're off at their nightly supervised dinner in a nearby building. At 5:30 P.M. (just when most kids are getting wild with hunger), they stuff down burgers and hot dogs, then quickly adjourn outside to play. In bad weather they go to the resort's recreation room, a large, unadorned shed that contains pool and table tennis and an immense video library that includes numerous classic children's titles.

Most activities at Goose Cove Lodge are centered around its natural setting. Marked hiking trails reach every corner of the property, and most weeks there's at least one guided hike. Or you can guide yourself with the trail map available at the front office. One popular hike crosses a sandbar to Barred Island, a Nature Conservancy preserve. Be sure to cross at low tide, however, for the bar is underwater at high tide. The lodge maintains a small number of rowboats and canoes suitable for brief, shore-hugging outings. For those unwilling to test the frigid Maine waters (which takes in most people, we would guess), there is no swimming opportunity at the resort.

Several nights a week the resort schedules after-dinner entertainment ranging from a piano player to a natural-history lecture to a movie.

Any family configuration can find suitable lodging here. Smaller families might choose a suite in the North or East Annexes located near the main lodge. Larger groups might prefer one of the 11 cottages, all of which have refrigerators or kitchenettes, as do a few of the annex rooms. All rooms also have fireplaces. They're furnished simply but tastefully in a mixture of modest antiques and good-quality tag sale items, with attractive prints and handcrafts for adornment. The baths are modern and functional. Every lodging is named after a wildflower or tree: Azalea, Kalmia, Periwinkle, Lupine, etc.

Fully as appealing as the lodge itself are its surroundings. Deer Isle is a lovely, unspoiled piece of Downeast landscape. A short drive from the lodge is the working lobstering village of Stonington, where you can catch fishing and sightseeing boats as well as the daily mail boat to Isle au Haut, a remote section of Acadia National Park. Elsewhere on the isle you can find fine crafts shops, including the Haystack Mountain School of Crafts. Mount Desert Island is about an hour and a half up the coast.

Lighthouse Inn

West Dennis, MA 02670
508-398-2244
Open late May through October

Lodging: 61 rooms in cottages, motel units, and lodges; all with private bath, television, phone, and small refrigerator; some with living room and fireplace.

Rates: $67–$105 per person per day, MAP; children, $25–$40 per day depending on age. Rates slightly lower in June, September, October.

Facilities: Ocean beach; heated pool; 2 all-weather tennis courts; putting green; shuffleboard; miniature golf; recreation room with pool table, video games, and table tennis.

Family amenities: Supervised children's morning program, lunch, dinner; evening children's entertainment; swingset.

The Lighthouse Inn may be one of Cape Cod's best-kept secrets—a compact, beautiful, lovingly run small beachfront resort that goes to great lengths to accommodate children. Its proprietors, the Stone family, started the resort in 1938; the thoughtfulness of the operation reflects this long personal experience.

The resort comes by its name legitimately: the center section of the white clapboard main lodge was built in 1850 as a lighthouse to mark the breakwater of the Bass River. The light, though no longer of much use navigationally, is still lit every night.

The inn occupies 7 acres of pristine beach property, with green lawns framed by scrub pines and shore roses. The cottages and

Photo by Nancy P. Metcalf

The main inn and lunch balcony.

lodges are in the classic Cape Cod style—weathered gray shake siding, white trim, and rose trellises. The Stones spend part of each winter haunting auctions and flea markets in search of furniture for the cottages. The inviting result is rooms that really do look like your own living room. The rooms all have wall-to-wall carpeting and some sort of outdoor private area—a terrace, a balcony, or a small lawn. Families would probably be happiest in one of the motel suites or cottages since these accommodations have at least two rooms.

Predictably, the two waterfront cottages come at a premium, but it's really not necessary to have one since no point on the property is out of sight of the ocean, or more than a couple of minutes' walk from it. Yet for all its compactness, the resort property doesn't feel crowded, perhaps because of the expansive ocean and sky.

A large stone breakwater that's really not suitable for swimming takes up most of the 700-foot waterfront. But on each side of the breakwater is a small beach for wading or sunbathing. Bordering the property on the west is a very long town beach.

Because West Dennis fronts on Nantucket Sound, the surf here never gets particularly high. Also, a tendril of the Gulf Stream passes by the Lighthouse Inn, making the water a comfortable swimming temperature quite early in the season. We saw remarkably little man-made debris on the soft sand beach. The waterfront has a gentle slope quite suitable for toddlers.

The solar-heated pool is also well configured for small children. It's 3 feet deep at the shallow end, with a recess containing underwater benches on one side, and a similar recess with broad, shallow steps on the other. A parent can easily sit in either spot with an infant or toddler, while keeping an eye on older children swimming in the deeper parts of the pool (most likely in the company of several Stone grandchildren).

A few steps outside the pool enclosure is a rudimentary but functional miniature golf course and a sandy beach-side lawn used for children's games and volleyball.

Every summer the Stones hire a staff member to oversee a children's program that runs literally from breakfast until bedtime. In the morning and afternoon there are organized games and play, inside or out, wet or dry depending on the weather, for ages 3 through about 9. If the parents want to take off for a day of adult shopping and sightseeing, the kids can have a supervised lunch as well.

In the huge, wood-paneled ground-floor recreation area of the main lodge there's a closet bursting with games, art supplies, and a full stock of outdoor games and sand toys. For older children the recreation area offers a pool table and an alcove of video games. On our visit it was a magnet for adolescents.

The kids' program continues with an optional supervised children's dinner table and after-dinner entertainment, also in the recreation room. We saw *An American Tail* on a projection TV one night, and a live magician another. While the kids were enjoying this fun, adults began trickling down from dinner to order drinks from a small bar. They sat around talking, while the older kids drifted over to the pool table. Yes, the recreation area is big enough to encompass all this after-dinner traffic.

Meals are taken in a high, airy dining room on the main floor of the lodge. In contrast to the familial relaxed quality of the rest of the place, dinners are rather more formal. Women and girls must wear skirts, and men, ties and jackets. The menu features competently prepared standard American dishes—roast beef, corn on the cob, scallops, and the like. Kids' portions are available.

Lunch can be taken either in the main dining room or on the breezy deck outside, no more than 30 or 40 feet from the water's edge. A poolside snack bar serves burgers, hotdogs, fries, and sandwiches. Kids can eat here in their bathing suits, seated at kid-sized tables and chairs.

West Dennis sits squarely in the middle of the Cape's south shore, with fairly easy access to pretty much any mid-Cape destination you'd care to visit. But, frankly, we'd just as soon stay right at the inn, away from the traffic and congestion, smelling the roses and watching the sea.

Oakland House

Sargentville, ME 04673
207-359-8521
Open early May through October

Lodging: 10 rooms in Shore Oaks lodge, 7 with private bath; 3- and 4-bedroom suites in Acorn annex; 15 cottages sleeping 2–8, with bath, living room, kitchenette, some with fireplace.

Rates: $287–$609 per person per week in August, MAP. Rates lower in July, lowest in June. Add $28 per person per week for full AP. Housekeeping rates in spring and fall, $225–$475 per cottage per week. Children's summer rates: up to 2 years, $42 per week; ages 2–5, half adult price; 6–11, two-thirds adult price.

Facilities: Ocean waterfront and boat dock; lake beach; tennis court; rowboats; badminton; croquet.

The Littlefield family has occupied this stunning property on Eggemoggin Reach for more than 200 years. In 1889 the saltwater farm began receiving summer visitors. Except that the guests now arrive in cars instead of steamboats, and enjoy indoor plumbing and electricity, it has changed very little in the past century.

Oakland House's pleasures come pure and simple. They do not derive from fancy accommodations—while clean and comfortable, Oakland House's cottages are far from luxurious, and its recreational facilities are rudimentary. Rather, the joy of a stay here emerges from the unforced decency of the staff, the gentle tempo of the daily routine, the spacious and unspoiled natural surroundings.

Bring your family here if you like your Maine coast straight, without tchatchke shops, video arcades, factory outlets, and fast-food restaurants. Sargentville is a wide place on a narrow two-lane blacktop road on the Blue Hill Peninsula in East Penobscot Bay. Just an hour down the coast from traffic-clotted Mount Desert Island, the peninsula remains amazingly undeveloped, with just a few summer homes, crafts workshops, antiques stores, farms, and fishing communities.

Families at Oakland House stay in one of 15 cottages scattered widely throughout the grounds. Some are down by the water (early risers often spy seals sunning on the rocks), and some are tucked into the wooded hillsides above. Built over the course of many decades, the cottages range from very rustic log cabins to modern bungalows. The Littlefields will send you detailed written descriptions of each to help you make your choice. All have kitchenettes where, if you elect the Modified American Plan, you can manage simple lunches. One consideration to keep in mind: some of the cottages are at the opposite end of the property from the dining room, too far for very young children to comfortably walk.

Meals are taken in the Italianate Victorian main house, originally the farmhouse. This has been scarcely touched over the years; the elderly furnishings and wallcoverings have long since faded to sepia hues, and the floors tilt satisfyingly. Dining tables are set up in several of the downstairs rooms as well as a summer annex built off the back. With its whitewashed low-beamed ceiling and wrap-around screen windows opening onto flower beds, this is our favorite dining location. In very hot weather the Littlefields put a hose on the tin roof and let water run over the eaves. You have the pleasing sensation of eating inside a waterfall. (This is, incidentally, the extent of Oakland House air conditioning.)

The food is basic and fresh, served on blue-and-white china and white tablecloths. There are two entrees at each meal and, always, some kind of delectable home-baked muffin or biscuit.

Just outside this building is a broad lawn suitable for croquet or badminton, and a cracked and weedy ancient clay tennis court. Except as brief diversions, these are beside the point.

What's very much to the point are Oakland House's two beautiful pieces of waterfront—a half mile on Eggemoggin Reach, an arm of

The main house.

Penobscot Bay; and a 600-foot beach on a 2-mile-long freshwater lake, Walker's Pond, on the other side of the property.

The oceanfront, a classic Maine landscape of pebbly beaches and boulders, is no more than a few minutes' walk from any cottage. The water is so frigid it makes your feet numb to wade in it (although it's said to warm up in August enough so that very brave swimmers venture in). Our children found a great deal to do there, especially at low tide. They clambered on the rocks, chilled their toes in the water, picked up various interesting pebbles and shells.

Still, the quiet lakefront is a welcome contrast. Its narrow sandy beach and shallow, clear, warm water make it perfect for children of any age. We spent an idyllic afternoon there catching immense polliwogs and watching youngsters from a neighboring boys' camp frolic on their swimming float. The lake is a rather long hike from most of the cottages; we preferred the short car ride.

The resort maintains a few rowboats at both the lake and the saltwater dock. However, for boating we recommend taking one of the many cruises, ferries, or mailboats leaving from various nearby harbors. The Oakland House office has stacks of brochures on all these.

Oakland House makes a point of not organizing guest activities.

The "scheduled" events are an occasional video movie shown in the old barn, and the weekly beachfront lobster supper. This is not to be missed. It starts with homemade fish chowder and proceeds to fresh lobsters, perfectly cooked (along with burgers and hotdogs for non-lobster-eating children). Guests find a perch on a rock and watch the sun set while they eat.

It's perfectly possible to spend a time-stands-still week just reveling in Oakland House's peace and quiet. But we suspect children—especially of school age—might tire of this after a bit. Luckily, there's plenty to do within an easy drive. Mount Desert Island and Acadia National Park are a mere hour away. The working fishing village of Stonington lies on Deer Isle, across the bridge to the south, and from there you can catch a ferry to Isle au Haut, a remote section of Acadia that's relatively uncrowded even in mid-August.

On the peninsula itself, the lovely town of Blue Hill is worth a trip, if only for a visit to Blue Hill Books, where you can buy autographed copies of Robert McCloskey's classic children's books such as *Make Way for Ducklings* and *Blueberries for Sal* for the cover price. McCloskey summers nearby and stops in periodically to sign a new stock of books. To complete your children's literary tour, ask a local to point you to the house where E. B. White, author of *Charlotte's Web*, lived for many years.

Sebasco Lodge

Sebasco Estates, ME 04565
207-389-1161 or 1-800-225-3819
Open late June through early September

Lodging: 64 rooms in main inn and lodges, all with phone, private bath; 7 small cottages with 1–2 bedrooms, living room, phone, some with fireplace and kitchenette; 13 family cottages of 2–6 bedrooms, phone, living room, kitchen, some with television and fireplace.

Rates: Inn and lodge rooms, $69–$79 per person per day, double occupancy; small cottages, $76–$92 per person per day, double occupancy; family cottages, $172–$382 per day for minimum occupancy of 2 persons, $38 per day for additional person over 12; children under 2, $16 per day; 2–6, $22 per day; 7–12, $28 per day, all MAP.

Facilities: Heated saltwater pool; 9-hole golf course; putting green; bowling green; 2 all-weather tennis courts; gift shop; candlepin bowling alley; recreation room with table tennis and video games; canoes, sailboats, paddleboats, motorboats; shuffleboard. Additional charges for golf, tennis, and boats.

Family amenities: Supervised children's program for ages 4–7 daily 9:30–11:30 A.M.; outdoor playground.

Sebasco may well be the only medium-sized, not too fancy, full-service family resort on the Maine coast. Its 700-acre Casco Bay property crammed with recreational facilities, its summer calendar spilling over with folk concerts, boat rides, lobster picnics, barn dances, and bingo games, Sebasco offers families a busy vacation at a very reasonable price.

With its 1950s vintage decor and homey but well-kept grounds, Sebasco lacks the tasteful, sophisticated airs that many newer, more expensive resorts affect. But for folks who do not care about architectural detailing so long as their cabin is roomy, sturdy, and clean (and we wager this category includes most children under 12), this is a place to consider.

In spite of its acreage, most facilities on the resort are located within an easy walk of each other. Unless you are staying at one of the few outlying cabins, you can park your car for your entire stay and forget about it while you take advantage of Sebasco's many recreational assets, which include:

• An enormous heated saltwater pool built on a rock outcropping in the bay. Floating on your back, you gaze out at Maine scenery while luxuriating in Florida water temperatures. The pool is only 2 feet deep at the shallow end; we saw a 19-month-old child wading comfortably there. The deep end has a diving board with a safe 10 feet of water underneath. The pool is fenced off from the rest of the grounds and a lifeguard is on duty during the day, both to watch the swimmers and to dispense beach towels and pads for the sturdy wood lounge chairs.

• A small but well-kept 9-hole golf course, complete with pro shop and snack bar. During the high season—from early July to late August—the resort charges a very reasonable greens fee of $42 per week (carts are $6 per 9 holes, but on this compact course you don't really need one). Early or late in the season there's no extra charge for golf.

• A substantial piece of the incomparable Maine coastline, in this case an inlet leading out to Casco Bay. Rent a motorboat or join one of the daily cruises on the resort's boat, the *Ruth*. One day it might be a seal-watching outing, another day a trip to an island picnic.

• A long and diverse schedule of organized daily events: aerobics classes, softball games, musical performances, square dances.

And that's not even counting the many activities Sebasco puts on just for children. Every morning from 9:30 to 11:30, for the ridiculously low fee of $3 per child, you can drop your 4- to 7-year-olds at a playhouse supervised by one of Sebasco's gung-ho college-age employees. The playhouse is a big octagonal building, originally a dance hall, now stocked with toys and games. In good weather the kids are taken to the nearby playground furnished with a good-quality wood swingset and climber.

Children might also enjoy some of the resort's general entertainment, such as the clown-magician who performed during our stay, or the weekly "pirate trip" on the *Ruth*. Watch your kids' eyes widen when, midway through the hour-long expedition, a fierce-looking "pirate" boards the boat.

Older children seem drawn to Sebasco's funky recreation building. This barnlike structure houses a four-lane candlepin bowling alley with automatic pinsetters that occasionally actually work. (Candlepins are a kind of bowling found only in this part of the country. The pins are tall and cylindrical instead of pear-shaped, and the cantaloupe-size ball has no finger holes. It's light enough that even preschoolers can propel it down the lane.) There's also table tennis, bumper pool, and a small lineup of video games. This

A guest cottage and lodge.

Photo by Nancy P. Metcalf

building is open 7 to 10 nightly as well as on rainy days; you can leave your preadolescents there without fear.

Outdoors, school-age children might be interested in the manicured lawn bowling court, the tennis court, or the shuffleboard courts. A freshwater pond on the property is too weedy for swimming but is a pretty place to take the canoes or paddleboats moored at its edge.

The management orchestrates all these activities with a practiced hand. On your arrival (normally Saturday afternoon), you're handed a sheet listing every activity scheduled for the coming week and told whether, and how, to sign up for it, and how much extra it costs (if anything). On Saturday night all guests are invited to a welcome reception featuring a bountiful hors d'oeuvres buffet. This is a sociable resort, where guests expect to get to know each other.

Sebasco is essentially two separate resorts as far as lodging is concerned. Its Georgian-style main inn, as well as several smaller inn-type lodges, cater to adult guests. Families are assigned to one of the numerous individual cottages on the grounds. Some of these are basically living room-bedroom combinations with tiny kitchenettes. The ones we liked best were in the thick of the resort, a few steps from the waterfront and pool. But large families on tight budgets, or families with children too young to be allowed near the water, might prefer the Pinecrest cabins set back in the woods. These have full kitchens and a common yard that has its own swingset. One cottage, Shore Ledges, has six bedrooms and baths, an ideal setup for a multigenerational family gathering.

Breakfast and dinner are served in the main dining room, a somewhat featureless but clean and pleasant large space in a postwar building set well back from the shore. The menus, served by waiters and waitresses, feature standard American dishes distinguished mainly by the freshness of the ingredients, particularly the fish and produce. There's no children's menu but the food is basic enough that picky eaters can probably find something to their taste.

On your walks around the resort, be sure to pause and admire Sebasco's many beautiful perennial garden beds. Interest in them has run so high that Sebasco arranges regular organized garden lecture-tours, and the plants are labeled.

Over the course of the week Sebasco feeds its guests in several interesting venues besides the main dining room. Sunday mornings it rolls an authentic-looking chuckwagon down by the pool for an outdoor waterfront breakfast buffet. Other special meals include a lobster picnic at a nearby beach and a steak barbecue in a pine grove on the resort grounds.

You are on your own for lunch. If you have a kitchen or kitchenette you can fix something there. Or you can throw a tee-shirt over your bathing suit and walk a few hundred feet from the pool to the snack bar, a comfortable, unpretentious spot overlooking the water. Make sure to sit out on the screened porch if the weather is nice. The menu is straight lunch-counter American: burgers, chips, egg salad, BLTs, and ice-cream sundaes at prices that went out of style elsewhere about 10 years ago. This is the real version of what upscale city diners are trying to imitate.

With so much activity on site you really don't need to leave the resort to find something to do. But in nearby Bath you can visit the new, architecturally striking Maine Maritime Museum (Sebasco will pay your admission if it's a rainy day), and the famed Freeport factory outlets are about a half-hour's drive south. With its usual thoroughness, Sebasco will provide you with a list, updated weekly, of events and sights in the area.

Rock Gardens Inn
and Cottages

Sebasco Estates, ME 04565
207-389-1339
Open mid-June through September

Lodging: 10 cottages of 2–4 bedrooms, all with fireplace and deck or porch; 4 rooms with private bath in main house.

Rates: $66–$86 per person per day, depending on cottage occupancy; $52 per day for children under 10; special rates for children 3 and under, all MAP.

Facilities: Recreation building with table tennis; croquet; horseshoes; full use of all Sebasco Lodge recreation facilities and programs (see previous chapter).

Family amenities: Access to all Sebasco Lodge children's programs and events (see previous chapter).

The property of this small cluster of cottages on a peninsula jutting out into Casco Bay used to extend back to the land now occupied by Sebasco Lodge. When its owners sold that land to Sebasco's original developers, they made sure that guests at the Rock Gardens Inn would always have full use of the larger resort's facilities.

Now, three owners and many years later, this unusual arrangement has left Rock Gardens Inn with a pleasing dual identity: a quiet, intimate seaside cottage colony with gorgeous 180-degree ocean vistas, and a full-service resort with many recreational assets.

Photo by Nancy P. Metcalf

A guest cottage.

The cottages are immaculate and airy, with whitewashed board walls and miscellaneous summer-camp furnishings, all in excellent repair and many spruced up charmingly with calico cushions, braided rugs, and patchwork quilts. Every cottage has at least a partial view of the sea, and several have magnificent ones, along with porches or decks from which to enjoy them. The cottages do not have kitchenettes, but guests have access to communal refrigerators and ice machines in several huts set strategically throughout the grounds.

The center of the colony is the main building, which includes the lobby and sunroom-library, site of the inn's only television as well as of books and games for rainy days. It's also the location of the soothing, informal dining room, with its blue-painted chairs, white linen tablecloths, burnished wood floor, and bouquets gathered from the gardens that bloom throughout the resort. The peninsula is so exposed to the sea that there are few trees here, only shrubs and green lawns ending in rock outcroppings at the shoreline.

The feel of the resort—tranquil and pristine, but not intimidating—seems to reflect the tastes of its young owners, Neil and Ona Porta, who live here year-round in a beautiful new shingled house built smack in the middle of the property (guests who don't know it's a private house are always asking to rent it).

Rock Gardens guests tend to socialize with one another, making use of Sebasco only for their active pursuits. If you prefer an atmosphere of calm and quiet to Sebasco's more bustling one, this might be your choice. Be aware, however, that it's about a 5-minute level walk for a brisk-stepping adult between Rock Gardens and Sebasco, and a considerably longer walk with children in tow.

Weekapaug Inn

Weekapaug, RI 02891
401-322-0301
Open mid-June through Labor Day

Lodging: 58 twin-bedded rooms with private bath, some with daybed sitting area; 8 single and 2 double-bedded rooms in teenage suite on top floor with shared bath.

Rates: $15–170 per person per day, single occupancy, $135–$150 double occupancy, AP. Children's rates, $30–$80 depending on age and room size and location.

Facilities: Ocean beach with bathhouse and snack bar; 2 all-weather tennis courts; shuffleboard; lawn bowling; croquet; pond, boating beach with kayaks, canoes, Sunfish, rowboats, windsurfers; rental bicycles; library; TV room; games and puzzles; bottle club-lounge.

Family amenities: Supervised program for children ages 3–12 operating mornings, lunchtime, and dinner; playroom with bumper pool and table tennis; swingset.

The Weekapaug Inn is a well-kept secret within a well-kept secret. This stretch of the Rhode Island shore, between Connecticut and Newport, contains white sand beaches and ocean surf that rival those found anywhere else in the Northeast. But perhaps because it's deceptively easy to get to, or because the summer residents here tend to be rich and discreet, the area has never been a big tourist magnet. The Weekapaug Inn is a jewel of a small beachfront resort hidden

The inn.

deep in a colony of fabulous shingled turn-of-the-century "cottages" in the midst of this area.

As you might suspect, a week's stay at this place costs a breath-taking bundle. Advertised by word of mouth only, the inn generally attracts moneyed people of quiet manners who fit right into the local scene.

Owned and operated by the Buffum family since 1899, the inn was originally located on the barrier beach. The great 1938 New England hurricane destroyed that building. The current inn opened a year later at its present location, a large, flat peninsula jutting into a big saltwater pond in back of the barrier beach. Water surrounds it on three sides, giving practically every room a water view.

From the outside, the inn is a rather ungainly barnlike structure sheathed in the same weathered shingles that enclose all the other buildings in the cottage colony (somewhat prosaically called the Weekapaug Fire District). The rear of the building, overlooking the lawn, tennis courts, and pond, has deep decks and porches fur-nished with comfortable chairs.

Nothing about the exterior prepares you for the inside. With public rooms on two levels, connected by a broad central staircase, it resembles nothing so much as an aristocratic private club. Most of the furnishings and decor date back to (or predate) the building's construc-tion; the Buffums have apparently decided (and correctly so) that something so perfectly suited to its role needn't be gratuitously changed.

Fine antiques (including a magnificent grandfather clock) are everywhere as are comfortable sofas and chairs, but nothing overly flashy or stylish. It just wouldn't be in keeping, you know. The main sitting room, a huge second-floor space, is decorated to match its name, the Sea Room, with pale aqua seat coverings, walls, and carpet. This is the setting for bingo, dancing, guest speakers, and movies. There is also a wood-paneled sitting room, the Pond Room, with chintz-covered furniture, Persian rugs, and a small bar where guests can mix their own drinks from their private stock stored in a small adjoining locker room.

How, you might ask, would parents with young children ever manage a cocktail hour of any kind? By taking advantage of the inn's well-run children's program, that's how. From 5:30 to 8:30 nightly the children's director oversees an early children's dinner. Afterward, the kids might play on the sturdy new wood climber on the lawn or enjoy a video in the ground-level children's playroom.

The same facilities are used for the morning portion of the children's program, which begins right after breakfast and ends just after lunch. In sunny weather the staff takes the children to the beach where they splash and play games until it's time for a picnic lunch. They might also take a nature walk, hunt for shells, or do some arts and crafts. The morning session costs $10 per child, and the evening session, $8.

Though the main beach is just a block down the road from the inn, the staff much prefers to take the children in cars to Fenway Beach perhaps a half mile away. That's because with its steep dropoff and frequent strong undertow, the main beach is unsafe for young ones. In contrast, Fenway is protected by rock outcroppings with a gently sloping sandy bottom and waves that break well offshore with no undertow. On a hot August day it teems with blissed-out, sand-covered kids.

The Weekapaug Inn is so proper that guests are (politely) requested not to walk through public rooms in bathing suits, even with cover-ups. Instead, they're to change in the beach bathhouse where they can also pick up towels and rent sand chairs.

The inn's small stock of Sunfish, canoes, kayaks, and rowboats is kept in good repair under a small boat pavilion on the saltwater pond behind the tennis courts. "Pond" hardly does justice to this large, calm body of water where waterskiers and sailboats abound on bright, breezy days. There's also good clamming in its shallow parts.

Lodgings here are surprisingly simple—airy rooms with ruffled white tiebacks, white bedspreads, painted wallboard, and a few 1940s-vintage tables and chairs. The baths are small, elderly, and immaculate. A few of the rooms can connect into suites, while several are double-size, the extra space being devoted to a seating area with a daybed. These rooms have ample space for rollaway beds or cribs. On the top floor are ten rooms—eight with single beds and two with doubles—with a shared bath which the inn rents at a deep discount to the teenage children of guest families.

Every meal here is an event, and rightly so. The ground-floor dining room is as simple and genteel as the rest of the place with bentwood chairs and white linen tablecloths. Breakfast is the usual gargantuan resort selection, including the rarely encountered shirred eggs. Lunches consist of overflowing buffets of seafood, sandwich materials, composed salads, fruits, desserts, soups, and one or two hot entrees. You can also order three kinds of box lunch: sandwiches, fried chicken, or fruit and cheese.

Dinners are served at table. The five-course menus feature very ambitious entrees, the sort we think of as "protein with X and Y" — flounder with bananas and almonds, chicken breast with pecans and raspberry sauce, veal chop with oyster mushrooms and cognac. Thursday dinner is a pondside cookout with steak, chicken, fish, corn on the cob, and baked potatoes.

A short drive west from Weekapaug is Watch Hill, an elegantly funky resort town with lots of useless, charming touristy shops and restaurants and a working antique carousel. Still farther west, into Connecticut, is Mystic Seaport, a recreated nineteenth-century whaling village with an actual whaler the kids can climb over and into, and Mystic Aquarium, which has regular dolphin-and-seal shows and an amusing display of penguins.

Family
Country Inns

FRY 1991

The Inn at East Hill Farm

Troy, NH 03465
603-242-6495 or 1-800-242-6495
Open year-round

Lodging: 60 rooms, including 7 cottages with 2 bedrooms and 4 cottages with 3 bedrooms, a motel building, the main inn building, and Grandmother's Attic, a luxury 3-room suite. Kitchen in cottages, air conditioning and refrigerator in Grandmother's Attic rooms only.

Rates: $378 weekly, $54 daily per adult; no charge for children under 2 in same room with adults; $129.50 weekly, $18.50 daily per child 2–4; $259 weekly, $37 daily per child 5 through high school; $189 weekly, $27 daily per additional child 5 or older in family of 5 or more; all AP. Holiday and weekend packages available.

Facilities: 2 outdoor, 1 indoor pools; infant-toddler wading pool; small pond with boating, fishing, paddleboats on premises; inn-owned dock, swimming, and boating area at Silver Lake, 12 miles away; whirlpool and sauna; tennis court; game room with video games and pool table; farm buildings with livestock; volleyball; softball; shuffleboard; hiking trails. Winter—indoor skating rink; cross-country ski trails, rentals, instruction.

Family amenities: Supervised children's activities scheduled at least once a day in summer and over Christmas and February school vacations; babysitters available with advance notice.

If you're looking for something yuppified, posh, or pretentious, then pass up the Inn at East Hill Farm. If, however, you're looking for a place your kids will never forget, make your reservations today.

This family resort at the foot of Mount Monadnock is a patchwork of buildings—1950s-type cottages with knotty-pine furniture and the smell of the forest in them; chintz-curtained rooms in the inn proper; motel-type rooms with bland furniture but a great view; so-called "deluxe" rooms with air conditioning and refrigerators—scattered throughout the grounds of a working farm.

At the height of the summer season the inn caters to families with young children and, surprisingly, to elderly people. On our visit a handicapped couple were among the guests and the inn's staff were making every possible accommodation for them. They were given first-floor rooms and were helped in and out of the pool.

People come back here year after year with their kids. It's easy to see why. The place has the relaxed, comfortable, warm feeling you'd like your own home to possess.

Kids want—and are encouraged—to explore. The place is full of the kinds of nooks and crannies they love. There are a number of barns and lots of animals, including saddle horses, work horses, ponies, goats, pigs, fowl, dairy cows, cattle, and sheep. You can gather eggs from under a hen, milk a cow, ride a pony, and feed baby chicks right out of your hand.

There are also plenty of the more traditional resort activities: outdoor and indoor swimming pools (one of the outdoor pools has a slide), lawns for softball and volleyball, a horseshoes pit, a small swingset, a wading pool for little ones, and hiking trails. You can row or paddle a boat either at the small pond on the inn grounds or at the inn's lakefront beach on Silver Lake, about a 12-mile ride away.

The staff are mainly college-age kids, uniformly wholesome, handsome, and helpful. And for all its lack of pretense, the inn is thoughtfully arranged and managed.

For instance, the shop in the main building contains the sorts of things people might forget to pack—toothbrushes, batteries, etc.—as well as a small but excellent selection of paperback books (including nonpotboilers), a few well-chosen examples of local crafts, and things to keep kids occupied, such as junior-sized fishing rods, cards, and bead necklaces.

The inn takes an unusual approach to organized children's programs. Although there is no fixed period of babysitting or supervision, each day contains several appealing activities. Children might visit the barns first thing in the morning to gather their breakfast eggs (if they hand-carry the eggs to the kitchen, the chef will cook them up on the spot). Late morning might bring a scavenger hunt, an ice cream-making session, or a talent show. Arts and crafts might be on the afternoon agenda, followed by a story hour. Young helpers are always welcome for late-afternoon cow milking, perhaps followed by a pony ride. The inn also has an outdoor children's wading pool and a pleasant playground. Together these things make the resort especially appealing to preschool and young school-age children.

Adult entertainment isn't neglected, either. Grown-ups are equally

The barnyard.

Photo courtesy of Inn at East Hill Farm

welcome in the barns, and the resort has a bring-your-own cocktail hour every night. Many evenings feature adult-oriented entertainment—a bingo game, live music. And every day, from 3 to 6 P.M., the resort thoughtfully reserves one of the outdoor pools for adults only.

Once a week the resort puts on an all-day beach party at the Silver Lake facility. You can take a ride on a speedboat, try your luck at waterskiing, fish for bass and trout, or just enjoy the dock, the diving float, or for the little ones, the shallows near the shore. There are dressing rooms and restrooms on the site.

The inn specializes in first-rate country cooking—good, wholesome food and plenty of it. Most meals are sit-down affairs in the large central dining room. The large menu includes many healthy choices—yogurt, salads, sensational homemade soups and breads, poultry, and fish—in addition to your basic meat and potatoes. The kitchen crew is always willing to cook up a hamburger or hot dog for kids who don't like anything else on the menu. The inn keeps a fresh pot of coffee on hand all day, and next to it a pile of homemade muffins and other pastries for between-meal snacks, a blessing for parents with 6-year-olds who turn ravenous at 3 P.M. Occasionally lunch is served buffet-style in a screened-in building next to the main inn, and eaten on picnic tables on the lawn.

Summer is the main family time at the resort, but some athletic families also enjoy the inn in the winter, when it becomes a cross-country ski resort. There are organized children's activities during the Christmas and February school breaks. Nonskiing youngsters can ice skate in the indoor rink, or on the pond if there's not much snow—the inn has a large supply of child-sized skates for rent.

The Inn on Lake Waramaug

North Shore Road
New Preston, CT 06777
203-868-0563
Open year-round

Lodging: 23 rooms in main inn and guest lodges; all with private bath, cable TV, phone, air conditioning; some with fireplace. Some rooms connect to form suites.

Rates: Weekends, $112–$132 single per night, $154–$194 double per night, MAP. Midweek, $104–$122 single, $138–$156 double, MAP. $45 for children under 12 sharing room with parents, MAP. Rates lower November through June.

Facilities: Lake swimming beach; indoor pool; exercise room; whirlpool; sauna; canoes, rowboats, Sunfish; volleyball; dining room and snack bar; clay tennis court; game room with pool table, table tennis, video games.

Family amenities: Children's dinner seatings; children's portions.

Located on Connecticut's biggest natural lake about an hour's drive from New York City, the Inn on Lake Waramaug has many personalities. It's a romantic getaway for couples, a beloved local landmark, and—last but not least—a family escape. Balancing all these roles isn't easy, but innkeepers Kevin and Barbara Kirshner do a pretty good job of it.

Lake Waramaug has been a summer retreat for more than two centuries. Set in the gentle green Litchfield Hills, its winding shoreline is heavily built up with lovely summer cottages, many of them now lavishly restored and enlarged by wealthy New Yorkers. The pretty country towns nearby abound with elegant antiques stores, chic restaurants, and bookshops. Don't come here expecting untrammeled wilderness. This is a more domesticated country experience.

The inn's eighteenth-century main building has served continuously as a hostelry since 1795; a plaque in the dining room documents the chain of ownership since then. Recently bought by an investment group which hired the Kirshners to run the place, the inn has undergone considerable refurbishing, with more to come. The several cozy public lounges are beautifully done with period furnishings, Persian rugs, and meticulously restored and painted wainscoting, bookshelves, and mantelpieces. Look closely, however, and note with relief that there's nothing about that small hands can ruin. Kids can play a game of Uno or Parcheesi in one of the living rooms and attract nary a disapproving look.

The rooms upstairs in the main inn, of assorted shapes and sizes, all have reasonably modern private baths and period-style furnishings, which might include four-poster beds and comfortable wing chairs. Families, however, will probably prefer the two detached motel-style "guest houses," a short and easy walk from the main building. Their rooms are very big—each holds a double bed, a single bed, a seating area, and usually a fireplace—and have large, modern baths. Several of them connect to form suites that can easily contain a family of six. The decor is similar to the rooms in the main lodge.

Meals are taken in the spacious dining room attached to the main inn. Furnished with beautiful old tables and chairs, burnished wood floors, and pink chintz curtains, it's an elegant setting for equally elegant French food. There's no children's menu, but the inn makes an effort to seat families early, at a distance from childless diners, and will cut down entrees to child-size portions and leave out the fancy parts. The adult filet mignon with foie gras and bearnaise sauce becomes, for children, an unadorned but tender and tasty steak.

Photo by Nancy P. Metcalf

The main inn.

In the summer ask to be seated on the roomy dining porch just off the main dining room. It's shaded with a high canvas tent top and looks across the inn's woodsy grounds.

In terms of recreational facilities, this is definitely an inn and not a destination resort. There's a single clay tennis court and a small but usable bathing beach on Lake Waramaug. The sandy shore slopes gently out for about 25 feet but then drops off abruptly. Luckily, the lake bottom changes from sand to muck at just that point so your kids probably won't want to step there, but care is called for nevertheless. The inn keeps a few rowboats, canoes, and Sunfish pulled up onshore for guests to use as they wish, and there are plentiful lounge chairs. Thursdays through Sundays a small lakeside snack bar serves up light lunches and munchies; the building also contains restrooms.

Many kids, ours included, far prefer the surprisingly large oval indoor pool housed in a sunny, barnlike addition to the main building. Somehow this manages to avoid that steamy, chlorinated feel that afflicts so many indoor pools. We also like the safe, yet not rough, footing provided by the pebbled concrete pool decking. Up on a balcony overlooking the pool are a small collection of exercise equipment and a recreation room with a couple of video games, a pool table, and table tennis.

If you possibly can, visit the inn during one of its locally famous special-event weekends. Most of these make use of the property's immense front lawn sloping gently down to the lake, and several are uncommonly clever. There's a January winter festival featuring snow sculptures and ice skating, a mid-March maple-sugaring festival using the inn's own trees, a frog-jumping jamboree in early July, a festival of bagpipe music and Scottish dancing in August, a Huckleberry Finn homemade raft race over Labor Day weekend, a pumpkin-carving contest in early October, and—most risibly— a "live turkey Olympics" the weekend before Thanksgiving. The famously dimwitted gobblers compete in the high jump, a weigh-in, an eating contest, and a running race. For humans, there's a best-turkey costume contest.

There are two good family day trips nearby. One is to Quassy, an old-fashioned amusement park in Middlebury. The other is a very short drive away in Washington, one of several towns that border the lake. The American Indian Archaeological Institute is a serious museum of Eastern Woodland Indian life and culture, a refreshing antidote to the myths and stereotypes your children have likely absorbed from school and television. Among other things, there's an authentically constructed Algonkian village with three wigwams, a longhouse, a rock shelter, and a garden planted with pre-Pilgrim crops.

Mountain Top Inn

Mountain Top Road
Chittenden, VT 05737
802-483-2311 or 1-800-445-2100
Open year-round

Lodging: 33 rooms in main inn, some of which connect to form suites, all with private bath; 3 cottages of 1–3 bedrooms, with fireplace, private bath; 5 bedrooms in farmhouse, with 3 half- shared baths; 19 homes with 2–4 bedrooms, fireplace or woodstove, living room, dining area, fully equipped kitchen or kitchenette.

Rates: $238–$332 per adult for 2-night minimum stay, MAP. Children's rates for shared accommodations, ages 2 and under, no charge; 1–6, 35 percent of adult rate; 7–16, 50 percent of adult rate. Rates higher on winter weekends, lower in June, September, early October, lowest in late October, November, mid-March through May.

Facilities: Summer—Heated outdoor pool; lake beach; canoes, rowboats, pontoon boat, Sunfish, rowboats with motors, windsurfers; fly fishing with instruction in stocked ponds; horse stables with trail rides, lessons; all-weather tennis court; 5-hole pitch-and-putt golf course; mountain bikes; claybird shooting; putting green; shuffleboard; croquet; badminton. Winter—110 km cross-country ski trails; cross-country ski rentals, shop, lessons, and clinics; snowshoe rentals; horse-drawn sleigh rides; outdoor ice-skating rink with skate rentals; tobogganing and sledding; sugarhouse. Year-round— Game room with pool table, table tennis, foosball, and speed

hockey; cocktail lounge; sauna and whirlpool; gift shop; videotaped movies; parlor board games.

Family amenities: **Children's menu; children's cross-country ski equipment rental and instruction; pony rides for children under 7.**

Think of the Mountain Top Inn as a small country inn with the recreational facilities of a very big resort. Also take its name very literally: this homey complex of buildings really does sit on 1,000 acres on top of a mountain a few miles outside of Rutland, with a sensational view across Chittenden Reservoir to the Green Mountains.

If there is another place this size in the Northeast with as much to do as the Mountain Top Inn has, we are not aware of it. Moreover, everything, but everything, is included in the price of admission—daily one-hour trail rides, mountain bikes, cross-country ski clinics, motorboats, things that normally cost extra. In the summer virtually the only things not covered in the daily rate are the optional $15 three-day fishing licenses, lunches, and whatever you choose to imbibe from the cocktail lounge.

The main inn building is a large farmhouse-like structure perched on the side of a hill. Below it spread the pool, the small but entertaining golf course, and, a short drive or long walk down the hill, the Chittenden Reservoir and its bathing and boating beach. All public rooms and many of the guest rooms have expansive lake and mountain views. The main sitting area of the inn has a big, welcoming stone fireplace and many clusters of comfortable, Colonial-style chairs and sofas. Guests tend to hang out here, leafing through the magazines or newspapers scattered about or playing one of the board games piled on a side table.

The rooms in the main lodge are large and tastefully though not luxuriously furnished with Shaker-style and antique pieces. Some function as bed-sitting rooms with queen-size beds and fold-out sofas. These would serve well for a small family; larger families might prefer a connecting pair of rooms. A short walk up the hill from the main lodge are three "cottages" that also offer very flexible family accommodations. Each cottage has two large bed/sitting rooms with private baths which can be rented separately or as a connecting suite; and two of the cottages contain a small single bedroom, without bath, that can open onto either side.

The property also includes 19 privately owned vacation homes which are rented to inn guests when their owners are absent. They run the gamut of styles and sizes, but all are modern and attractively furnished. They have kitchens and can be rented with or without the meal plan. A caveat: they're so far from the main inn that occupants should expect to drive to most of the recreational facilities. In fact, this property is so big, and its facilities so widely scattered, that you'll need your car occasionally no matter where you stay.

The final and most economical lodging option (a 20 percent discount from regular rates) is a large, clean, but plainly outfitted farmhouse at the very top of the property. With five bedrooms and three and a half baths, it's a good choice for large families or groups. It looks out on the resort's stocked trout pond (novices can take fly-fishing lessons here) and a small herd of cattle kept "just for the heck of it," according to Bud McLaughlin, who owns and runs the place along with his wife and her brother and his wife.

Though the Mountain Top Inn doesn't go in for organized children's activities, kids of most ages will keep happily busy here.

The lakefront has a big, sandy beach on a protected cove that keeps it warm and calm even on breezy days. The beach slopes

The main inn.

Photo by Nancy P. Metcalf

gently into the water, ideal for babies and toddlers. Set a few yards back from the beach are a split-log changing house; a recreation building with restrooms and table tennis; a small, staffed pavillion stocked with cold drinks, snacks, life jackets of all sizes, and balls, birdies, and racquets for the volleyball and badminton nets set up on the sand. Canoes, small motorboats, rowboats, windsurfers, and Sunfish are available for guest use. Also moored here is the inn's pontoon boat, which once a week ferries guests to a wooded lakefront peninsula for a breakfast picnic. Because the beach is located at the bottom of a long, steep dirt road leading down from the main inn, all but the hardiest guests will probably drive to it.

Older children might prefer to swim in the heated, kidney-shaped pool perched on the hillside a few yards away from the main inn. Comfortable beach chairs furnish the brick surround, and there's always a pile of fresh towels on hand. When they tire of swimming, the kids can nip over to the nearby shuffleboard or croquet courts. The innkeepers are also very tolerant of youngsters crashing around on the all-weather tennis court; they even keep a stock of well-used old racquets in the ground-level, walk-out game room for just this purpose.

Guests should also not fail to take advantage of the inn's terrific equestrian facilities. The livestock barn houses 25 well-trained horses and opens out onto a practice ring. Twice a day in the summer, the equestrian staff lead one-hour rides around the inn's extensive network of trails. Children ages 7 and up are welcomed on these rides and even provided riding helmets of the correct size. Our 7-year-old, who had never steered a full-size horse in her life, had a wonderful ride. The attentive young staffer made sure she got a gentle horse and put her in line right behind him. Kids younger than 7—but old enough to sit on top of a horse without sliding off— get about a 15-minute walk up the road and back, with a staffer on foot leading the horse. Families with serious riders might consider the inn's special equestrian clinics, which include daily riding lessons; instruction on horse care, physiology, and health; and up to six hours of riding per day.

In the winter the inn turns to another unusually intense specialty: cross-country skiing. Bud McLaughlin boasts that the inn has the best cross-country skiing in the Northeast, and he may be right. This tiny place maintains 100 km (67 miles) of well-marked, mapped trails, including 2 ½ km with snowmaking. It is an official training center for the U.S. Nordic Ski Team, and its school is directed by a three-time Olympian and former coach of the U.S. Olympic Nordic Ski Team. The inn's winter rates include free equipment and free daily lessons for all ability levels, from complete novices to advanced competitive racers.

Winter sports enthusiasts who aren't bushed after a day on the trails can take a spin on the inn's lighted outdoor skating rink, plunge down the hill behind the inn on a sled or toboggan, or glide through the snow on a horse-drawn sleigh pulled by the inn's huge draft horses.

No matter what the season, guests will be astounded at the quality of the inn's food. The low, beamed-ceiling dining room, on the ground floor just beneath the main lounge, is simply but handsomely furnished with cane-seated chairs and wood tables (the high chairs are tall, narrow versions of the regular chairs). The menu looks standard enough—pasta, seafood, chicken, and beef entrees for dinner; soups, sandwiches, and salads for lunch; eggs, pancakes, and waffles for breakfast—but the ingredients and preparation are superior. Our seafood chowder had chunks of very fresh lobster, fish, and bell pepper in a satiny cream base that betrayed not a hint of cornstarch thickener. Our filet mignon was perfectly tender, perfectly pink, and covered with an impeccable bearnaise.

Children get their own menu, printed on the same heavy paper in the same elegant script as the grown-up version. The chicken, hamburgers, and grilled cheese are prepared with the same attention to quality as the more complex adult fare. The French fries are homemade; the fruit cup holds the freshest of seasonal strawberries and blueberries.

Suits-Us Farm

Box 89
Bovina Center, NY 13740
607-832-4369
Open Memorial Day through Columbus Day

Lodging: 13 single rooms, 22 2-room family suites in main barn, Carriage House, and Chicken House, all with private bath. Largest suites sleep 6.

Rates: Barn, $285 per person per week, double occupancy; children $70–$170 a week depending on age. Chicken House and Carriage House, $260 per person per week; children $55–$145. $55 per week additional for 2-room family suites. Daily rates also available. All rates AP.

Facilities: Outdoor pool; lighted all-weather tennis court; practice backboard; basketball court; recreation room with table tennis, video games, board games, TV with video library; hiking trails; hayrides; farm animals; fishing pond.

Family amenities: Playground.

When they bought these 355 acres in the improbably beautiful northwestern Catskills, Alexander and Elisabeth Rabeler planned to keep dairy cows and raise market vegetables, just like their neighbors. But farming, then as now, paid poorly, so to make ends meet they started taking in guests from the New York City area in 1956. One thing led to another, and today the Rabelers preside over a good-sized farm-resort. Nowadays the animals are borrowed from nearby farms for atmosphere, and the produce is raised elsewhere.

Nevertheless, Suits-Us Farm still looks and feels very much like a real farm, not a simulated one. You can tell by the rusting agricultural vehicles parked at the edges of fields, the genuine fake wood paneling in the guest rooms in the converted barn, the faint smell of animals, the gas pump sticking up between the house and the barn, and the complete absence of wood hearts or twig wreaths.

Perhaps that is why it attracts such a wonderful cross-section of New Yorkers of every ethnicity and economic level. Some are bemused to find themselves vacationing at a place so unselfconsciously rural, with basically not much to do, but they return again and again nevertheless.

Perhaps they are responding to the easy camaraderie that develops during the long, lazy evenings in the dining room-cum-game room on the first floor of the barn. Perhaps they relish the freedom to walk down a deserted road, look across a green field, feast their ears on absolute rural silence. Or perhaps they merely regard their children, liberated from Riverdale apartments to roughhouse on the endless lawns, or fish in the stocked pond. When we arrived, we found three children deeply involved in making a fort out of two folded-up lounge chairs. This is no frenetic Catskill resort, but a place that still retains the rhythms of its origins.

The senior Rabelers are semiretired benign presences now. The main work falls to their two sons, Lawton and Frederick, and their daughter, Monica Farley, all of whom are industrious and friendly, in an unforced way. Except for a hayride or two and a weekly barbecue, they pretty much leave guests to their own devices.

Appropriately enough, the barn is the center of action here. Built in 1918 of massive posts and beams, it was converted into lodging in the early 1970s. In virtually every room parts of the original beams remain exposed. The Rabelers put lots of insulation between rooms and floors. In bed at night you feel embraced by the building's solidity and silence. On both lodging floors the rooms open onto large central sitting areas where parents can quietly converse, read, or play cards after the kids have gone to bed.

The furnishings are in keeping with the farm's unfashionable rural esthetic: our suite contained green industrial carpeting, an ancient oak dresser, a rickety bedside table, a 1950s table lamp that listed to one side—and an exquisite antique brass bed that would fetch a small fortune in a Manhattan shop. Like any frugal farm

Photo by Nancy P. Metcalf

The barn.

wife, Elisabeth Rabeler accumulated the furnishings at local auctions and estate sales. She just did it on a larger scale than usual.

Two outbuildings, named after their original functions and located just a few yards from the barn, also contain rooms or suites outfitted like those in the barn. The rough-hewn exteriors of all three lodgings have been altered as little as possible except for the necessary windows and doors.

A short walk uphill from the barn are the outdoor recreational amenities. The pool is large and deep enough for a diving board and waterslide. There's a nice playground with a swingset, a merry-go-round, and a bunch of tractor tires half-buried in the ground to climb on.

Back toward the woods are assorted pens, sheds, and small barns housing the farm's borrowed animals. Children are invited to troop along for the 5:30 P.M. feeding. They help scatter lettuce in the pen housing the sheep and goats, stop to pet the new golden retriever puppies, try their hand at milking the cow, and wrinkle their noses as the young farmhand slops the pigs who live in a muddy depression at the base of a hill.

Indoor activities center on the truly enormous ground floor of the barn. Except for the kitchen, it's a continuous open space. And surrounding it on two sides is an enclosed porch of at least equal size. Several dozen mismatched dining tables don't even fill half of it. At one end of the porch is a recreation area with table tennis and video games. In a cranny in the main space are a bunch of chairs and sofas clustered in front of a television with a large video library stacked next to it. A closet contains all kinds of board games and art supplies.

Hung high on the walls and set on ledges about the barn are a fascinating assortment of old tools and farm implements Elisabeth accumulated over the years. The scythes and rug beaters are recognizable, but can you identify a coal strainer or the thing that used to pick up bales of hay out of the loft?

After dinner's cleared away, the guests hang out in the barn and interact. One night we recorded these simultaneous goings-on: kids watching a video, kids drawing Ninja Turtles on a piece of posterboard, kids playing cards, a mother and sons playing Boggle, two women weaving tiny wreaths and bracelets from straw they'd collected during an early evening hayride, adults playing chess, adults playing cards, and a father and son playing table tennis.

Meals at Suits-Us are fit for a hungry fieldhand. Breakfast features eggs and pancakes cooked to order, or you can get your own cereal from the jumbo-size boxes set out on the buffet. Lunch is also served buffet style and features a huge and bewildering assortment of fresh-cooked food and leftovers: soup and chowder, casseroles, beans and franks, summer-fresh sliced tomatoes, and sublime chocolate chip cookies were one day's offering.

Dinners are hearty single-menu affairs that tend toward meat, potatoes, simply prepared vegetables, fresh salads with one of several excellent homemade dressings, and still more delectable home-baked goodies. We still get misty over the memory of Monica's cinnamon rolls. The waitress brings platters and serving bowls to your table and you help yourselves. Every table gets its own carton of milk—waxed cardboard for small families, plastic gallon jugs for bigger ones.

Between meals the Rabelers set leftover desserts behind a glass door in a pantry, along with a plentiful supply of milk and coffee. People vow they'll stay away, but minutes later are irresistibly drawn to the Rice Krispies-marshmallow squares and crumb cake.

This part of the Catskills is far removed from the touristy section further south. However, there are a couple of excellent day-trip destinations nearby, including Howe Caverns and the Baseball Hall of Fame in Cooperstown.

Wildflower Inn

Darling Hill Road
Lyndonville, VT 05851
802-626-8310
Open year-round

Lodging: 15 bedrooms and 5 suites in main house and 2 outbuildings. Main house bedrooms have shared baths; all others have private bath. Some rooms have kitchenette, washer-dryer. One room equipped for wheelchair access.

Rates: $80–$125 per room per night, double occupancy, B&B. Fall foliage rates slightly higher, midwinter rates slightly lower. Additional adults in same room, $10 per night; children ages 6–11 in same room, $5 per night. Children 5 and under stay free.

Facilities: Heated outdoor pool and wading pool; spa and sauna; TV room with VCR; marked cross-country ski trails.

Family amenities: Children's game and dress-up room; play area with climber and sandbox.

Located only a shortdistance off I-yet very much out in the country, the Wildflower Inn has such a comfortable, familial ambience that guests might almost feel they are visiting friends. The proprietors, Mary and Jim O'Reilly, parents to six young children, especially welcome families not only to beds and breakfasts, but to their extensive property, where horses graze in the fields, ducks populate the pond, and rabbits wander freely over the lawn. In the rooms, various memos to guests ("Ten Things to Do on a Rainy Day," a mapped-out "Sunday Drive") reinforce this sense of solicitous yet unforced hospitality. This is, in short, a rarity among country inns: a place where families with children can feel entirely at home.

The setting of the Wildflower Inn is one of extraordinary beauty, above a deep valley with the Green Mountains in the distance. Patios and terraces overlook the mountains and the swimming pools; lush lawns are bordered by neat flower beds. The road which runs past, though smooth and entirely navigable, is unpaved. The neighboring properties are working farms.

Within this setting, the inn itself is charmingly old-fashioned yet comfortably renovated. Rooms have been inserted in the original farmhouse, a former carriage house, and a former schoolhouse on the property. Each room is decorated with its own wildflower theme, expressed in stencils, curtain fabrics, and dried flower arrange-

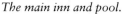

The main inn and pool.

Photo courtesy of Wildflower Inn

ments. Some rooms feature Colonial furnishings—four-poster beds, patchwork quilts, and the like—while others are somewhat more contemporary.

Suites offer accommodations most suitable to families with children, since they include bunkbeds and other extra sleeping space, as well as well-equipped kitchenettes with dining areas. The Family Suite can hold up to eight people; the Meadow Suites each sleep four people.

The O'Reillys suggest that rooms in the main farmhouse itself may be most convenient for parents of very young children. The dining room, sitting room, and TV room are downstairs in this building, permitting adults to put children to bed and then descend for evening conversation and relaxation while remaining within earshot (or baby-monitor range) of the children.

Preschoolers and young school-age children will find many things at the inn solely for their amusement: a toy room in the farmhouse stocked with games and a trunkful of dress-up clothes; a shallow wading pool full of water toys and inflatable rings; a play area with playhouse, climber, and sandbox; a barn and duck pond to explore; and perhaps a hay- or sleighride, depending on the season. It must be said, however, that the available pleasures are simple and rural in nature and might not hold the attention of older children. As noted above, the inn has but one television. There are no video games, pool tables, or other big-kid amusements.

Further afield, the O'Reillys are pleased to direct you to local lakes and mountains for fishing, skiing, or hiking; to nearby museums, antiques dealers, a cheese factory, a maple sugarhouse, a bowling alley; golf courses both full-size and miniature; and all sorts of shops.

Meals at the Wildflower Inn are served in a beautiful glassed-in porch overlooking the valley. Breakfasts are of egg and pancake heartiness; cold cereals, fruits, and fresh baked goods are also on hand. Children may order "teddy bear" pancakes. Also included in the room rate is an afternoon snack in the sitting room, with tea, lemonade, cookies, crackers, and cheese.

Dinners are served at additional cost Tuesday through Saturday; reservations are needed. Entrees are of the good Continental restaurant variety: veal cutlet, ribeye steak, spinach tortellini.

Portions are generous and the quality is adequate for the setting. The children's menu offers the usual standbys: hamburgers, grilled cheese, fried chicken.

In the absence of a specific recreational plan such as bicycling or attendance at some regional festival, a traveling family would seek out the Wildflower Inn for its beauty and serenity; to show the children a bit of country life; and to sleep through a night whose only sounds are those of crickets and birds.

Winter Clove Inn

Round Top, NY 12473
518-622-3267
Open year-round

Lodging: 35 rooms in hotel, 15 rooms in 2 motel units, 3 rooms in small lodge, all with private bath.

Rates: $70 per day, $420 per week, AP; children ages 3 and under, no charge; 4–16, $3 times child's age per day, 5 times daily rate per week.

Facilities: Indoor and outdoor pools; river swimming hole; marked and mapped hiking trails; all-weather tennis court; 9-hole golf course; putting green; snack bar; game room with pool and table tennis; 6-lane bowling alley; 15 km marked and groomed cross-country ski trails; ski rentals; volleyball.

Family amenities: Seasonal activities including hayrides, picnics, barbecues; swingset; babysitting available on one day's notice.

In an area where many older resorts have gone to seed or become terminally tacky, the Winter Clove Inn has managed the neat trick of updating its programs and facilities without losing the simple country virtues that made this part of the Catskills one of the nation's earliest vacation destinations.

On top of that, it's a terrific bargain. A family of four, including school-age children, can spend a week here for under $1,200— including three abundant meals a day.

The inn's spectacular 400-acre mountainside property has been

Photo by Nancy P. Metcalf

The main building.

in the Whitcomb family since just after the Revolutionary War. The family has operated the property as an inn for 127 years. The unusual name comes from a small valley—a cleft or clove—so deeply shaded that it remains snowbound well into the spring.

After a winding drive past many lesser resorts, your first view of the inn is its lovely main building, an impeccably maintained four-story white frame structure graced by a long, cool, arcaded porch.

The inn rooms are large and freshly kept, with four-poster beds and modernized private baths. The downstairs public rooms, with their dark fake-wood paneling and floral wallpaper, present a somewhat perplexing blend of modern synthetic blandness—Herculon plaid sofas—and the elegance of bygone days—massive antique chests and ornate woodwork. In any event, there are no doodads or delicate furnishings about to tempt your children or make you nervous.

The motel units are somewhat more private, though convenient to the main building. And the three-room suite over the bowling alley is very modern and ideal for large multigenerational gatherings.

Meals are taken in the large, plainly decorated dining room and feature American fare—pork roast, pancakes, and the like.

The real attraction is the inn's natural setting and recreational facilities. The outdoor swimming pool is a bit deep for preschoolers but fine for older children. It's fenced and surrounded by lots of comfortable lounging furniture. Our kids far preferred the large indoor pool, which is not quite so deep, with steps spanning the entire width of the shallow end from which they hurled themselves happily into the water for one entire evening.

Older kids and young adolescents might appreciate an improbable amenity—a fully operational six-lane bowling alley directly across from the main building. The lanes also incorporate a snack bar, a pool table, and table tennis.

The property slopes steeply upward from behind the inn. On the first rise up is a small 9-hole golf course—nothing fancy, but a pretty spot for a leisurely afternoon's play. Use of the course is free, but you'll have to bring your own clubs and do without electric carts. There's also a single hard-surface tennis court.

The inn's biggest asset, however, is the network of hiking and cross-country ski trails that depart from its back door. The Whitcombs have thoughtfully prepared a map of the trails, complete with descriptions of features along each, and pictures of animal prints and trees you can expect to encounter along the way.

One short loop takes you to a covered footbridge from which you can look down over a small but steep waterfall. Another path leads you to an idyllic swimming hole at the bottom of the falls. A beautiful day hike ends up at a mountain lake where you can eat your picnic lunch (the kitchen will put a huge one up for you) and take a dip, then explore the ruins of a nineteenth-century hotel and the Otis elevator that carried guests up to it. Other trails pass by old quarries, abandoned charcoal pits, ledges offering spectacular long views, even a natural bathtub carved in a mountain stream. Warning: these hikes are somewhat strenuous and probably best undertaken by older children or by well-conditioned parents carrying babies in backpacks. Preschoolers and young school-age children would probably find them too demanding.

The same trails serve for cross-country skiing in the winter. The inn has a supply of rental skis.

Being located in the middle of the Catskills, the inn is naturally surrounded by every kind of tourist attraction imaginable—water parks, railroads, horseback-riding stables, and the like. It borders on a distant edge of the Catskill Game Farm, a sizable zoo worth a half-day's visit. Be aware, however, that this is not a modern zoological park. The animals are mainly confined to small fenced enclosures, although the game farm's managers claim to maintain breeding herds of several rare species of African antelopes. Be sure to take a cooler of water; otherwise, you'll have to slake your thirst with flat, lukewarm soft drinks on sale at inflated prices.

A Place
at the Lake

FRY 1991

Alden Camps

RFD 2, Box 1140
Oakland, ME 04963
207-465-7703
Open late May through early September

Lodging: 18 cabins with 1–3 bedrooms; all with private bath, screened porch, woodstove, lake view.

Rates: $360–$510 per person per week, double occupancy, AP. Rates lower with more adults in cabin. Children's weekly rates, age 1 and under, $36; 1–3, $72; 4–6, $120; 7–9, $180; 10–11, $240. Rates lower before July 1, after Labor Day.

Facilities: Lake swimming beach; shared docks; rowboats and canoes; rental fishing boats with motors; waterskiing; clay tennis court; recreation barn with shuffleboard, table tennis; horseshoes; croquet; ballfield; lounge with library, board games.

Family amenities: Swingset and sandbox.

People have been coming to the Belgrade Lakes chain in Maine to fish for generations. Alden Camps, on the headwaters of the chain at East Lake, is an attractive, conveniently located (7 miles off I-95) traditional fishing camp which also happens to have terrific food and an easygoing, welcoming attitude toward kids.

In the center of the state not far from Augusta, the Belgrade Lakes have neither the wild grandeur of the more remote parts of Maine nor the cachet of the shore. They are merely clean, spacious, pretty bodies of water loaded with trout, bass, and pickerel, and perfect for swimming and waterskiing as well. E. B. White used to venture in from the coast to fish here with his son. Originally a lakeside farm (the farmhouse, much expanded, now serves as the main lodge and dining room), Alden Camps has taken in guests since 1910. Its elderly current owners, George and Vesta Putnam, are descendants of the founder, and for the last several years have left the operation of the camp in the energetic and capable hands of Wendy and Jerry Coons.

The camp layout is especially felicitous. The 18 cottages are spread along a footpath by the shore (no cars here; a staffer brings your gear down in a tractor-drawn cart), far enough apart for a bit of privacy but close enough together that everything's within an easy walk of everything else. Thus, every cottage has a lake view and a screened porch from which to enjoy it. All are within a stand of truly towering mature pines.

At intervals along the shore are wood docks where guests tie up fishing boats, either their own or the distinctive blue-painted Alden rentals. There were five such docks when we visited but the Coonses plan to install more.

Up a small incline from the cottages, overlooking a green playing field and lawn, is the plain clapboard main lodge. At one end is a comfortable living room, which opens up to a spacious, informal dining room. Across the entire side of the building is a deep screened porch amply supplied with rockers and tables. Just outside the door is a small children's play area containing a new wood swingset-climber and a sandbox stocked with outdoor toys. Restless children sometimes dart out to play between courses; after meals their parents can linger over coffee within sight of the children playing outside. On rainy days the kids invade a bin of toys kept under a table in the living room.

A few steps from the main lodge is the recreation barn. It is literally that—a huge and quite beautiful old hand-hewn post-and-beam barn with a solid concrete floor. It houses two indoor shuffleboard courts and table tennis, with 80 percent of the space left over for running around.

The cottages themselves are quite rustic, as you would expect in a place like this. They're made of rough clapboards or half-round logs with unfinished board interiors and cathedral ceilings. Furnish-

The main lodge.

ings run to antique bureaus, cane-seated rocking chairs, and painted side tables. The bathrooms have stall showers and old-fashioned double spigot sinks as well as propane space heaters for cool nights late in the season.

Fishing holds pride of place here; those blue boats can be spotted all around the big lake during the day, and the kitchen will clean and cook anything legal that's caught. But nonfishing family members can find plenty to do, too.

The lake is wonderful for swimming—cool but not uncomfortably chilly, clear, with a sand and rock bottom. At the end of the cottage path nearest the main lodge is a groomed beach with a roped-off swimming area perfect for very young children, with a gentle incline and plenty of sand for digging. The camp thoughtfully supplies several large inner tubes. And once a day staffers take guests waterskiing behind the camp's big motorboat, at no extra charge.

There is one clay tennis court, in reasonably good repair, and hiking trails lace the camp's 240-acre property.

Because most guests come here with a recreational agenda in mind, the management does not organize many activities. Guests themselves (many of whom know each other well after years of vacationing here the same week every summer) put together a laid-back variety of Trivial Pursuit, shuffleboard, and table tennis tournaments, raft races, and singalongs, as the spirit moves them.

Normally, food in a fishing camp like this tends to the basic American variety, nourishing but forgettable. Not so at Alden Camps, thanks to an imaginative, risk-taking chef named Joe Plumstead. The menu, posted on a big blackboard just outside the dining room, contains the likes of sauteed lamb, smoked salmon, shrimp, lobster-crab Newberg, quiche, vegetable-cheese melts, twice-baked potatoes, grilled fish, and garlic-cheese bread. The homemade pastries—Irish soda bread, cinnamon-raisin muffins, blueberry pie—are uniformly excellent. Every meal is an adventure, especially now that Joe has taken to wintering in Thailand, where he's picking up the basics of that savory national cuisine.

Most guests come to Alden to stay put, but there are several day-trip destinations within an hour and a half or less: the Bath Maritime Museum, the L.L. Bean and outlet stores in Freeport, and whitewater rafting on the Kennebec River.

Attean Lake Lodge

Jackman, ME 04945
207-668-3792 (summer) or 207-668-7726 (winter)
Open mid-May through September

Lodging: 18 lakefront log cabins; most with 2 bedrooms; all with bath, porch, and fireplace or woodstove.

Rates: $90 per person per day, $450 per week; $150 per couple per day, $825 per week, AP. Children's rates, under age 5, no charge; 8–11, $40 per day, $190 per week; 5–7, $35 per day, $160 per week.

Facilities: Lake beach at lodge and along lakefront; canoes, fishing boats, and paddleboats; hiking trails; main lodge with puzzles, games, and books; swingset.

The Jackman area is a quiet backwater deep in the vast inland Maine landscape. It's your basic wilderness, the kind of place where a lake like Attean—clean, deep, and 6 miles long—can survive to the end of the twentieth century with a shoreline still almost totally undeveloped. A Canadian Pacific rail line runs by part of the shore, but save for once or twice a day when a freight rattles by, you wouldn't know it was there. What you notice instead are the mountains and the lake and the quiet.

To this setting the Holden family has welcomed guests since 1900. People come to fish, hike, hunt, and to feel, see, and smell nature. If you work at it, you can find the comforts and pastimes of civilization in nearby Jackman; but, frankly, if that's what you're after, why come at all?

Attean Lake Lodge is on Birch Island, a 10-minute boat ride from shore. Guests park their cars on shore, and their gear is ferried out

A guest cottage.

on a broad-beamed launch. The route to the island passes another small island with a cabin on it. This is the only other building on the lake.

Guest cabins at the lodge are handsome, rustic hewn log houses, cozy and comfortable, with broad covered porches and stunning views. There is no electricity in the cabins (a generator powers lights in the main lodge). Cabins are heated with woodstoves and lighted with kerosene lamps. Bring a couple of flashlights for nighttime navigation, and a battery-operated radio if you insist on continued contact with the workaday world. Every day the staff cleans the cabin, refills the woodbox and lamps, and brings in a new bucket of ice and large pitcher of spring drinking water. Not to worry, there are functioning bathrooms in each cabin (with normal hot and cold water). Cribs are available for infants.

Meals are solid fishing-camp fare, which is to say hearty and good. It's nothing especially fancy, but not just meat and potatoes either. Service is friendly, and the tables have linens and flowers. On Wednesday and Sunday nights the lodge holds a beach cookout. On other nights typical entrees might be baked manicotti, broiled steak, or American chop suey. Fresh biscuits or muffins accompany your breakfast eggs or pancakes, and cheese omelets appear regularly on the menu.

Because lodge guests tend to venture far afield during the day, lunch comes in picnic boxes filled with sandwiches, cookies, fruit, punch, or milk. There is no liquor service at Attean although guests are welcome to bring their own wine to dinner.

Activities at Attean are strictly individual affairs, which is how the guests like it. We encountered one family with school-age children that has returned for six years now. One day they'll pile in a boat and venture off to visit one of the dozen or so pretty natural sand beaches that punctuate the rocky, wooded shoreline. Another day they'll hike one of the many trails in the area. The Holdens stash canoes in various outlying ponds and streams so guests can create combined hiking and canoeing outings.

There is also a hiking trail on the island suitable for younger children. It can easily be negotiated in a half hour or less. In fact, the island is just small enough (and of course without cars) that kids can have a bit of freedom.

Many guests come to fish, naturally. Attean is a deep, cold lake abounding in lake trout, brook trout, and landlocked salmon, all sought-after game fish. You can buy a license at the lodge and rent fishing tackle if needed. If you catch something, the kitchen will clean and cook it. Canoes can be rented for $10 a day, aluminum fishing boats with small motors for $20 a day including gas and oil. The nearby Moose River and other streams offer fly fishing for trout or landlocked salmon as well.

A sizable sand beach near the lodge attracts lots of customers on hot days. The shallow water at the edge is fine for toddlers, and the lodge provides plenty of beach chairs, picnic tables, and sand toys.

The main lodge at Attean burned down several years ago, and two guest cabins were converted to serve as a temporary replacement. Construction on a much larger permanent lodge is well underway and scheduled for completion by the 1991 season.

Canoe Island Lodge

P.O. Box 144
Diamond Point, NY 12824
518-668-5592
Open mid-May through mid-October

Lodging: 63 bedrooms in main building, lodges, cottages, houses; all with phone, most with TV. Some units have fireplace, air conditioning, living room, and/or kitchen.

Rates: $442–$830 weekly per person, MAP. Children's MAP rates: ages 2 and under, $84 weekly; 3–6, $154; 7–12, $231. Rates include 3 meals daily before June 30 and after Labor Day.

Facilities: Swimming beaches on lakeshore and private island; 2 shuttle launches; waterskiing and windsurfing (additional fee, including instruction); 4 crewed sailboats; canoes, rowboats; lunch bar; 1 all-weather and 2 clay tennis courts; cocktail lounge; game room with large-screen TV, pool, table tennis.

Family amenities: Small playground; babysitting with advance notice; weekly family squaredance.

Ingeniously sculpted into a steep hillside plunging down to Lake George, Canoe Island Lodge is the personal, idiosyncratic creation of its owners, Bill and Jane Busch. Its crowning asset is its namesake, a pristine 4-acre wooded island in the middle of the lake, with a lovely picnic grove and a white sand bathing beach.

A lodge and lunch terrace.

The mainland side of the resort, where all lodgings are located, is crowded and hospitable, just the place for gregarious vacationers who want to spend a lot of time on the big, breezy lake and also have easy access to a bustling resort area. If you crave solitude surrounded by pure nature, look elsewhere.

Bill Busch bought this property in 1946 and over the years has expanded it—frequently with his own two hands—to encompass a startling variety of lodgings, most of them crafted from wood harvested from the hillsides that rise behind the resort.

You can opt for a luxurious cathedral-ceilinged suite, a fancy lakefront villa, a no-frills motel room, a three-bedroom cottage, or an actual log cabin. And that's just for starters. Whatever you need in terms of space configuration the Busches probably have, somewhere. The interior decor varies as much as the lodgings themselves, from brand-new and luxe to older and basic. Everything is clean and well-tended, however.

The mainland waterfront exists principally as a launching point for the resort's impressive fleet of sailboats and motorboats. The tiny beach next to the boathouse is crowded, noisy, and with its abrupt drop-off, dangerous for young children.

A large staff of college-age "boat boys" tends to all this marine equipment and operates the larger craft. If you don't know a yardarm from a mainsail, don't worry. The boat boys will handle the actual sailing of the lodge's new, custom-designed 30-foot red cedar boats. In busy times the boats sail on a regular schedule. Otherwise they depart at your mutual convenience. The boat boys also regularly take one of the lodge's big motor launches on tours around the long mountain-ringed lake.

For a small fee you can waterski or attempt to windsurf, both activities that might appeal to older children or adolescents.

One of the boat boys' most important tasks, however, is to shuttle guests back and forth to the island, which is as spacious and secluded as the mainland is crowded and busy. The ride takes only a few minutes in one of the launches (which are, by the way, equipped with life jackets for both adults and children).

After climbing out onto a broad, sturdy dock, you walk down a short wooded path to the sheltered south-facing beach, well-stocked with comfortable lounging chairs from which you can watch your children frolicking in the shallow, clear, sun-warmed water. Spend the entire afternoon here and feel the tension leave your body.

The shaded interior of the island contains plenty of picnic tables as well as sanitary facilities. Every Thursday night the lodge throws a chicken barbecue and songfest here.

In addition to the island, Canoe Island Lodge's other standout feature is its food. The menus look conventional enough—the usual American-Continental fare—but the execution is superior. Light, fresh-baked muffins and cornbread for breakfast, sensational apple crisp for lunch, blueberry pie for dinner; made-from-scratch soups and dressings; the freshest possible greens in the salads; the tenderest beef in the bourgignonne. You get the picture.

Breakfast and dinner are served in the main building's three huge dining rooms, all of which overlook the lake. Each family has an assigned table, and waiter, for the duration of its stay. For lunch you have the choice of the dining room or, in good weather, a lunch bar that opens onto a large, shaded outdoor dining patio over the boathouse, right next to the lake. If you have one of the cabins or cottages equipped with kitchens, you can prepare your own lunch.

Although the resort doesn't organize many activities specifically for children, kids have the run of the place. Downstairs from the dining rooms there's a rugged game room with table tennis, big-screen television, battered pool table, and table hockey where school-age children seem to congregate. Our kids, a bit younger, were fascinated by the indoor boulder—a rock outcropping so big that Bill Busch simply built the room around it rather than blasting it away. It rises from floor level to within a yard of the ceiling in one corner, at just enough of an angle to make climbing it fun yet reasonably safe.

On Wednesday nights the lodge puts on a squaredance in its big wood-floored ballroom that begins with a round of kids' games and dances.

Because of the steep terrain, the property is a little short on flat play areas. In fact, the children's play equipment and the tennis courts are across a busy highway from the rest of the grounds, and thus not very convenient. However, post-toddler children will probably be just as happy scrambling about the beautiful and complex network of stone stairways, bridges, and paths that connect the various resort buildings. These byways could, however, make hard going for younger children and strollers.

Its location in the thick of the bustling Lake George resort region makes the lodge a convenient jumping-off point for assorted trips. The splendidly honky-tonk village of Lake George contains bowling alleys, arcades, factory outlets, waterslide parks, and other rainy-day options. A bit farther down the highway in Glens Falls is the Great Escape amusement park.

Hemlock Hall

Blue Mountain Lake, NY 12812
518-352-7706 (summer) or 518-359-9065 (winter)
Open May 15 through October 15

Lodging: 8 rooms in main lodge, 5 with private bath; 11 cottages, studio–2 bedrooms, with bath and kitchenette; 4 motel rooms with private bath and small refrigerator.

Rates: $113 per person per day, MAP; $18 per day for children ages 2–8; no charge for children under 2. Rates lower May 15–June 15, Oct. 1–Oct. 15.

Facilities: Sandy lakefront beach; paddleboats, canoes, Sunfish, rowboats; mapped hiking trails.

Family amenities: Sand toys, child-size chairs, wading pool at beach; wood climber-swingset; children's board games in main lodge.

This pretty, secluded mountain resort started life as the Adirondack "camp" of a shoe magnate. The mansion, which sits atop a hill above the exquisite lake, retains its original 1898 detailing—burnished wood trim, chintz-covered windowseats, converted wall-hung gaslights, hooked rugs, marble bedroom washbasins, antique rustic twig porch furniture, massive stone fireplaces.

But Hemlock Hall isn't one of those museum-piece country lodges that might as well have a sign posted saying, "Children, do not touch." Paul and Susan Provost, the hard-working young couple who have owned the place since 1986, have made it a welcoming environment for all guests, kids included. On a warm

Photo by Nancy P. Metcalf

The boat dock.

summer night the children are apt to be having a rousing game of Pictionary or Parcheesi indoors, while the adults laze back in the porch rocking chairs, watching the stars, smelling the mountain air, and talking.

This is a small, uncomplicated resort most likely to appeal to outdoorsy families partial to fishing, hiking, and canoeing. You can, for instance, ask the kitchen to prepare a box lunch ($5 for two gargantuan sandwiches on homemade bread, a cooler jug of iced tea, and a big bunch of fruit in a sturdy rucksack), help yourself to a canoe, and spend a blissful day exploring the chain of three interconnected lakes that begins with Blue Mountain Lake. Or you can take one of the trail maps available at the main lodge and set out on a hike. One of the most interesting starts at the edge of the resort's parking lot and follows a valley to a beautiful mountain pond.

Down the hill from the main lodge is the swimming area, which looks across to a deserted, wooded island. The swimming area features a sunny, south-facing longish sand beach (scoops and shovels provided) fronting on a wood seawall. To enter the lake you descend a short flight of wood steps. At water's edge the lake is about 3 feet deep—too deep for very little ones—with a firm sandy bottom. For older children and adults there's a diving float further offshore. The resort does provide a plastic wading pool for very young children, whose water experience will probably be limited here. The water is a great advertisement for freshwater swimming —soft, cool, and clear.

A short stroll down the shore from the swimming area is the boating dock. Guests can use any boat free of charge. Children tall enough to reach the pedals seem to enjoy the light, maneuverable paddleboats. The nearby boathouse contains paddles and various-sized life jackets.

Your choice of lodgings at Hemlock Hall will affect your experience of the resort. Families strongly oriented toward boating might try for one of the units on the second floor of the boathouse, parts of which literally hang over the lake. But these are farthest from the main lodge, a somewhat steep uphill walk to breakfast and dinner.

Other units are scattered throughout the wooded, hilly grounds, although none is more than a 5-minute stroll to the main building. These detached cottages contain no-frills furniture and kitchenettes. Though clean, sturdy, and more than serviceable for families with rambunctious children, they're not high on esthetics.

The rooms in the main building, by contrast, feature lovely antiques and period architectural details. Families with very young children might find these rooms (the ones with a private bath, that is) preferable to a cottage because they can put the little ones to sleep and come downstairs for the rest of the evening at no more remove than they'd be in their own homes.

As you may have surmised by now, Hemlock Hall is no place for the private and reclusive. Everything about it encourages guests to get to know one another. Parents strike up conversations while watching their children at the beach. The kids play hide-and-seek on the porch while waiting their turn to ring the huge dinner bell. And, sitting around the picturesque living room or porch, adults tend to drift into the sort of intimate, soul-baring exchanges that seem to happen only when people are out of their everyday environments, with their guards down.

The Provosts have even arranged their mealtime routine to help guests get acquainted. A newer addition to the main lodge, the cozy, wood-paneled dining room is furnished with long tables that seat eight or more for family-style meal service (pass the mashed potatoes, please). Instead of staying at the same assigned table for the entire stay—the custom at most MAP resorts—parties are rotated to a new table at each meal.

The food isn't bad, either, especially served on the lodge's pretty Blue Willow dishes. Dinner consists of a single menu of basic American food (broccoli, baked chicken, sweet potatoes, and the like) dished out in large quantities. At breakfast you can have your eggs cooked to order and help yourself from an immense assortment of homefries, smoked meats, breads, and pastries. Guests prepare their own lunches in their cottages (the town of Blue Mountain Lake has food stores). In the evening the Provosts set out a tray of fresh fruit and a carafe of ice water for late-hour snacks.

In addition to the puzzles and board games available in the main lodge, Hemlock Hall has an incomparable rainy-day resource—the Adirondack Museum, which is literally around the corner from the resort. This state-of-the-art museum campus explores the fascinating history of the Adirondacks—its natural landscape; its explorers, miners, trappers, loggers, and sportsmen; its transportation; its wildlife. You can walk through a private Gilded Age railway car, peer into a one-room schoolhouse, or marvel at the ingenuity of a split-rail shack that sheltered an actual Adirondack trapper through a brutal mountain winter. In fact, don't miss this museum even if the weather's not rainy.

Loch Lyme Lodge

Route 10
Lyme, NH 03768
603-795-2141
Open Memorial Day through early September; main
lodge open year-round

Lodging: 24 cabins with 1–4 bedrooms; most with living
room, fireplace, and porch; 13 with kitchen or kitchenette. In
main lodge, 4 rooms with shared bathrooms.

Rates: $22–$35 per person per day B&B; $35–$48 per person
per day MAP. Children's rates range from no charge for
children ages 4 and under, to $18 for B&B and $23 for MAP.
Children stay free Sundays through Thursdays in June.
Housekeeping cottages $300–$475 per week, lower in early
June. Main lodge rates lower in fall and winter.

Facilities: Lake waterfront with beach and docks; rowboats,
canoes, and windsurfer; fishing; outdoor grills and picnic
tables; 2 clay tennis courts; badminton; volleyball; croquet;
game room with VCR, table tennis, and small library.

Family amenities: Children's playground; babysitting available with advance notice.

Proprietors Paul and Judy Barker say that most people come to Loch
Lyme Lodge to do nothing—and return year after year to repeat the
experience. For some families this small resort on New Hampshire's
Connecticut River border with Vermont is now a three-generation

tradition of rest and relaxation. But if your idea of a good time starts with tennis at dawn and ends with softball at dusk, you can also find it at Loch Lyme Lodge.

The resort is twice a post-world war phenomenon. Built in 1919, it features 24 rustic cabins scattered over a wooded hillside and down by the shore of the "loch" (Post Pond to locals). The main lodge, dating from 1784, provides B&B in four bedrooms year-round. Judy's mother worked as a dining room hostess at the lodge before her family bought the entire operation in 1946. Judy's father still tends the large garden that provides the kitchen with fresh vegetables throughout the summer.

Guests can choose between B&B or MAP cabins with living rooms and bedrooms, and housekeeping cabins rented by the week and equipped with kitchens or kitchenettes, picnic tables, and outdoor grills. Almost all cabins have porches, many screened, and fireplaces that are more than decorative on chilly New Hampshire evenings in early and late summer. Bathrooms run the gamut: shower-only, tub-only, or shower-and-tub. Every day cabin boys and girls clean up, make the beds, supply fresh towels, and restock the porch woodpiles.

Though not large the cabins have a roomy feel, with high, vaulted ceilings and simple furnishings. Our two-room, MAP cabin had a king-size bed and bureau in the bedroom, and in the living room a wicker chaise lounge, daybed, desk, and several wood bowback chairs. The effect is charmingly rustic, more reminiscent of Abe Lincoln than Leona Helmsley.

For families who opt for the economical housekeeping cabins, the lodge offers a one-time 50 percent discount on one meal Monday to Friday—and meal rates are low to begin with: $4.50 for breakfast and $13 for dinner for adults, considerably less for children. Don't pass up the opportunity. Loch Lyme Lodge meals are healthful, hearty, and delicious. The dining room has plenty of high chairs available and an atmosphere as informal as your own kitchen's. Indeed, the summer dining rooms serve for the rest of the year as the Barker family dining room, living room, and home office.

For dinner one night we had a salad of locally grown greens, warm pineapple bread, homemade cream of turkey soup, an entree choice of chicken, scallops, or pan-fried trout, buttered rice, carrots, and cauliflower. Dessert presented an agonizing selection from among hot fudge sundaes, several flavors of ice cream, maple Indian pudding, chocolate layer cake, strawberry shortcake. That's a typical Loch Lyme offering.

Breakfasts are similarly generous, featuring homemade muffins and buns, a fruit-and-cereal bar, and the standard selection of hot breakfast foods. A late sleeper? A self-service continental breakfast bar is kept open 9 to 10:30 A.M. Guests who've already breakfasted are invited to return for a second cup of coffee or bring the kids for a mid-morning snack. On Sunday nights guests can partake of a

A guest cottage.

Photo courtesy of Loch Lyme Lodge

lakeside buffet of hot and cold meats, salads, and entrees. For day trips the lodge will pack box lunches ($5 for adults, $3.50 for kids), and light snacks are available all afternoon.

Working up an appetite is no problem. The quiet lake is perfect for swimmers of all ages, including little ones who can paddle in the shallow water by the edge, and older ones who can venture out to the diving float. Rowboats and canoes are available for use at will; the daring or foolhardy can try a windsurfer (the lodge can arrange lessons). Two clay tennis courts and badminton, croquet, and tetherball gear are also on hand. We saw parents hitting fungoes with their kids on the baseball field, and if it's baseball talk you want, there isn't much Paul doesn't know about the Boston Red Sox.

The Barkers, parents of two young sons, have stocked ample play equipment for little ones, including swings, slides, jungle gyms, and balls. The lodge can also arrange for babysitters or mother's helpers.

Hiking trails abound nearby; the Appalachian Trail runs through neighboring Hanover. If you're in shape be sure to bring your bicycles to take in the picturesque scenery of the upper Connecticut River Valley: in Lyme itself; in Hanover, home of Dartmouth College, to the south; Orford, noted for its late eighteenth- and early nineteenth-century architecture, to the north; and, across the river, charming Norwich, Vermont.

For relaxation, white Adirondack chairs along the lake afford a view of water, green hills, sunsets, and children at play. Fishermen can pull pickerel, bass, and trout from the lake, and there are several golf courses nearby. The kitchen will clean and cook your catch for dinner.

For rainy days try the lodge's game room (a cabin aptly named Playwood), with table tennis, a television with VCR, fireplace, and small library. New in 1990 was a game Judy devised called Double-Digit Challenge for guests ages 10–15. Youngsters are challenged to complete 20 activities (from swimming a certain distance to writing a story), then to wait until the end of the season to see if they've won prizes.

Dartmouth's art museums and performing arts center, Hanover's movie houses, and the Montshire Museum of Science in Norwich also provide rainy-day getaways. Shopping opportunities include the huge Dartmouth Bookstore and legions of antiques dealers and flea markets. The kids might enjoy the weekly livestock auction in nearby East Thetford, Vermont.

The lodge's staff is remarkable for its diversity and friendliness. They're students recruited from colleges in the United States and Europe. On our stay we met young people from Scotland, France, England, Northern Ireland, Texas, North Carolina, and, of course, New Hampshire. In keeping with the family atmosphere of the lodge, Paul and Judy ask guests who are going sightseeing whether they're willing to take along an off-duty staff member. For youngsters—and adults—it's a great opportunity for an international experience in a decidedly Yankee setting.

Migis Lodge

P.O. Box 40
South Casco, ME 04077
207-655-4524
Open mid-June through early October

Lodging: 27 cottages, studio–5 bedrooms; all with color cable TV, fireplace, private bath, porch, lake view; some with wet bar and refrigerator.Main lodge, 7 rooms, some with shared baths.

Rates: $93–$104 per person per day, AP. Infants, $20 per day; half rate for children under 4 over the minimum occupancy for a lodging. Rates for children older than 4 vary according to location and capacity of cottages. Rates slightly lower in June and after Labor Day.

Facilities: 3 clay tennis courts; 3 lake bathing beaches; 2 shuffleboard courts; lake cruiser; sailboats, canoes, rowboats, and fishing boats with outboards; recreation hall with pool and table tennis; waterskiing; library and game room; walking trails.

Family amenities: Wood swingset; supervised dinner for preschoolers; babysitting available with advance notice.

This small resort on Sebago Lake, one of Maine's prettiest, has figured out how to be rustic and luxurious at the same time. It's possible to get close to nature here without forgoing superior food, attentive service, and handsome accommodations. Not surprisingly, Migis Lodge attracts a well-to-do, sophisticated clientele who appreciate its complex charms.

Visitors to Migis will not find much in the way of organized activities or any particular effort to get them acquainted with other guests. This is a place for enjoying the island-studded, 13-mile-long lake as you see fit, and savoring a rest time with your family. Meeting new friends is strictly optional.

This private atmosphere makes Migis a hospitable place for families even though it doesn't cater to children with many facilities or programs. For instance, there's no children's menu per se, but the excellent kitchen staff will whip up a hamburger or grilled cheese sandwich for a child who spurns the roast lamb, steak au poivre, or chicken moutard. For children too young to sit through a multicourse meal of any kind, Migis provides a supervised children's dining room that serves appropriate food in a hurry; the kids adjourn to the swingset to play while their parents linger over a swan-shaped eclair or hand-dipped chocolate-covered strawberries.

The quality and decor of its cabins distinguish Migis from many other lakeside cottage colonies of the same size and recreational variety. Tim Porta, the energetic owner, is slowly remodeling the cabins into a sort of slick-rustic style with burnished wood walls, floors, and furnishings, and stone fireplaces. The Arts and Crafts-style light fixtures and lamps were custom-made to Tim's specifications. Tim hires local craftswomen to hand-piece quilts and hand-braid wool rugs to match each cabin's color scheme. All but the tiniest cabins are being retrofitted with ceramic-countered wet bars and small refrigerators, perfect for storing snacks and baby food. These cabins could hold their own in a decorating magazine —quite a contrast to the haphazard castoffs one finds in many such resorts, even well-kept and relatively expensive ones.

Migis guests have access to the lake at many points along the resort's 1,900-foot shoreline. One bathing beach is reserved for adults; the water is deep there. A small protected cove at one end of the resort, and a much larger sandy beach at the other, are the preferred family venues. The larger beach has a stock of big inner tubes and inflatables for families who didn't bring these bulky items from home. Both family beaches have gentle, sandy sloped bottoms.

The resort takes a refreshingly relaxed attitude toward its good-size fleet of Sunfish, paddleboats, canoes, and fishing boats. Guests

Photo by Nancy P. Metcalf

A guest cottage.

can take the nonmotorized craft at will, from wherever they happen to be moored (the small swimming cove, for instance, usually has a couple of canoes pulled up on shore). To take a motorboat (for $15 a day, $10 a half day), guests need only sign their names to a book kept near the waterfront.

When the weather's right, Migis offers free waterskiing from the big boat dock in front of its sprawling main lodge. And every week Porta takes up to 20 guests on Migis' 35-foot lake cruiser on expeditions up the Songo River and over to Frye's Leap, a tall bluff overlooking the lake.

Otherwise, organized activities tend to revolve around Migis' meals, which, judging by the comments we heard, are one of the main reasons people return year after year.

Twice a week, for lunch Saturday and for breakfast Sunday, meals adjourn to a picnic grove on a small peninsula at one end of the property. It's fun to watch the staff serve these meals of grilled things with practiced skill. And eating off paper plates at a wood picnic table 5 feet from the water is a treat for kids. Wednesdays bring a steak cookout on Migis' 5-acre offshore island. The highlight of the week, however, is the awesome Saturday night buffet presented as elegantly as at the fanciest New York hotel. We tried to write down the offerings the night we sampled it, and failed miserably. We stopped counting the cold buffet offerings when we got to 27 (including cold lobster tails, assorted patés, salmon salad, hearts of palm salad, smoked oysters, deviled eggs, smoked salmon, shrimp, and blueberry gelatin). We think there were 13 desserts (strawberry mousse, fresh strawberries in a hollowed-out watermelon with an American eagle carved in its side, Key lime pie, and chocolate chunk cheesecake, to name a few). It's traditional to make a minimum three trips to the buffet: one for cold food, one for hot, and one for dessert.

In spite of the refined cooking and interior decor, however, you never lose the sense of being in the woods. Except for a little grass around the tennis courts and a sunbathing lawn in front of the main lodge, the grounds are left au natural, covered with ferns, pine needles, and very large trees. Chipmunks scamper across paths and under porches. Loons call from the lake.

Surprisingly, however, Sebago Lake is not far from civilization. A short drive from Migis' access road takes you to any kind of retailing establishment you're likely to need. And Portland is only about a half-hour away. On a rainy day you might take the kids there to the Children's Museum of Maine or the Maine Aquarium.

Purity Spring Resort

Route 153
East Madison, NH 03849
603-367-8896 or 1-800-367-8897
Open year-round

Lodging: Summer—45 rooms in cottages, a small inn, lodges. Winter—70 rooms including lodges at resort's King Pine Ski Area. Some rooms with private bath; some with shared bath; some cottages have fireplace.

Rates: Summer—$57–$66 per person per day late June through August, AP. MAP-only rates lower Memorial Day–late June and after Labor Day. Winter—$34–$68 per person per day, AP; $29–$63, MAP, in winter. EP only November-start of ski season and after ski season–Memorial Day. Summer children's AP daily rates if sharing room with 2 adults, ages 2 and under, $4; 3–7, $14; 8–12, $20.

Facilities: Summer—4 lake beaches; rowboats and canoes; mapped hiking trails; 5 tennis courts; shuffleboard; horse-shoes; badminton; basketball; library; cocktail lounge; croquet; VCR; game room with table tennis and pool; waterskiing; coin-operated laundry. Winter—King Pine Ski Area with 14 trails and 4 lifts; groomed cross-country ski trails; lighted night skiing; private and group ski lessons; ice skating.

Family amenities: Summer—Drop-in daily child care in club-house; supervised games, hikes, and arts and crafts programs; playground; babysitter roster. Winter—Children's ski lessons; day nursery at base lodge.

It's only 11 winding miles and 2 turns off the main highway, but the drive seems to take you back in time to the late 1800s, when Edward E. Hoyt turned an old farmstead into Purity Spring Resort.

Guests who make their way here will find a homestyle vacation spot steeped in tradition. As old as the grand hotels that once dotted the surrounding White Mountain region, Purity Spring has always eschewed their fancy trappings in favor of solid family accommodations, great meals, and all the activity that can fit in the great outdoors.

The Hoyt family and its many branches are still in full command at the resort, where they both live and work. Named for the pristine waters of the property's spring, the resort recalls its farm origins with its understated white clapboard buildings, trim lawns, radiant flower beds, and simple decor. Over the years the Hoyts have added tennis courts, groomed beaches for swimming in the clear lake, and included shuffleboard, basketball, horseshoes, hiking trails, and a porch for just plain sitting.

The emphasis is clearly on family fun. All four beaches are sandy with a safe, gradual slope; three of them have roped-off swim areas, making it easier for parents to keep adventurous children under control. Those inclined can explore the extensive lakeshore by rowboat or canoe or cast a line for pickerel, bass, or trout. If you clean your catch, the kitchen will cook it. Daylong guided hikes into the White Mountains are scheduled weekly, with day care at the resort's children's clubhouse for those too young to make the trip. On nonhike days the clubhouse and adjoining playground are open for supervised drop-in child care several hours a day so parents can enjoy a game of tennis or waterski from Sunset Beach.

Built on 1,400 acres of heavily wooded land, the resort has taken full advantage of its location. In the winter the Hoyts continue their family focus at the King Pine Ski Area, a bit down the road from the summer complex. This small area has four lifts (including a triple chair lift) and the same schedule of adult and junior ski clinics as much bigger places as well as an all-day nursery for those too young to ski.

The family-style dining room is part of the main inn building. Meals are informal and generous, with a good selection of tasty all-

The main inn.

American dishes—roast lamb, stuffed sole, steak, strawberry-rhubarb pie, carrot cake, homemade cookies, a salad bar, and made-to-order sandwiches. Breakfast is hot and abundant, in the best resort tradition. The servers are friendly and endlessly tolerant of young children; everyone seems to have worked here for years.

Downstairs in the main inn is the Cellar Door, the resort's indoor social center. There's a small bar open 5 to 10 P.M. (11 on weekends), a television, game boards, pool, and table tennis. It's the kind of place you don't mind taking an older child.

Rooms in the various lodgings tend to be functionally furnished with beds, bureaus, and a few chairs. If you take advantage of all the resort has to offer, you'll probably use your room for little more than changing clothes and sleeping, for which they're more than adequate. Portable cribs are available on request.

The accommodations are varied and flexible enough to suit any family configuration. There are rooms upstairs in the inn, in the adjacent Millbrook building that also houses the office, and in several lodges. The lodge rooms all have private baths and are grouped around common living rooms with televisions. Families with school-age children might find these appealing as they can put the kids to bed and adjourn to the sitting room for adult conversation and television viewing while remaining reassuringly close to their slumbering offspring. The lodges are also ideal for family reunions; ask the Hoyts about special group rates. There are also three cottages, two up the hill and one down by the lake. They have two units each, which can be combined into family suites.

Purity Spring employs a full-time activities director in the summer to organize a busy schedule of family and adults-only social events. These include scavenger hunts, a wine-and-cheese get-acquainted party, lake cookouts, volleyball games, campfires, skits and stunts, game shows, and table tennis tournaments. Everyone in the family can plan on making new friends.

If you can tear yourself away from the on-site activities, Purity Spring is located smack in the middle of the White Mountains' tourist attractions. Take the cog railway up Mount Washington, cruise the factory outlets in North Conway, visit one of the many theme parks, ride a scenic gondola, or hike into the mountains. Or, on second thought, stay put in the nineteenth century at Purity Spring.

Quimby Country Lodge and Cottages

Averill, VT 05901
802-822-5533
Open mid-May through September

Lodging: 20 cottages, studio–4 bedrooms; all with lake view, porch, woodburning stove; some with kitchen.

Rates: $95 per day per adult, AP; $85 per day semi-housekeeping (dinner only). Children under 3, no charge; 3–8, $50 per day; 9–15, $60 per day, AP; $40 and $50 per day, semi-housekeeping. Rates lower in early July and Labor Day week, lowest in May, June, September.

Facilities: Fishing pond with rowboats, canoes; swimming lake with 2 beaches, beach house with table tennis, windsurfers, Sunfish, canoes; recreation building with table tennis, indoor shuffleboard; 1 clay tennis court; main lodge with library, board games.

Family amenities: Daily organized activities for children ages 5–15; fenced playground; toys and games in recreation building; evening family games and parties.

According to its energetic managers, Marj and Stu Gear, only its refusal to displace longtime guests prevented Quimby Country Lodge from becoming the set for the movie *On Golden Pond*. We can understand what drew the film crew here. Quimby's 20 summer cottages have all the quintessential features: front porches with green-painted rocking chairs, slanty wood floors, tubs with feet, wicker furniture, hooked rugs, and charmingly mismatched antique beds and bureaus. Better yet, all this is perfectly preserved as part of a resort whose cleanliness, service, and imaginative programs rival those of much larger places.

Though small, Quimby is a "destination resort" if for no other reason than its near-total isolation on a 700-acre tract miles from a town of any size, at the very top of Vermont a few miles from the Canadian border. Not to worry, however. The resort is more than capable of filling up its guests' weeks with satisfying, wholesome activity.

Most of the resort's buildings are strung closely together on a low hillside along the shore of 70-acre Forest Lake. It's no more than a 5-minute walk on a broad, lighted footpath from the most distant cabin to the main lodge-dining room. On the way you can stop and admire the handsome flower beds that dot the grounds. Below the buildings, very near the lake itself, are the tennis court (site of a late-July round robin tournament dubbed "Quimbledon"), and a fenced playground containing a couple of swingsets, a jungle gym, a seesaw, and a sandbox. Forest Lake, small and somewhat weedy, has good fishing but isn't really suitable for swimming. You can explore it in one of the canoes or rowboats tied up to a dock in front of the main lodge, available free of charge for guests to use. The Gears will be happy to point out some rushy areas where kids can catch frogs.

The cottages themselves are white-glove clean and well-stocked with thick towels and washcloths, soap, stationery, and extra blankets. Some have unfinished pine walls; others are finished with old-fashioned wallboard. The semi-housekeeping units have basic kitchens. For families with infants in nonhousekeeping cottages, the resort will provide mini-refrigerators to store formula and baby food. Every porch has a hanging basket of flowers and a humming-bird feeder filled with red nectar. In keeping with Quimby's origins as a fishing camp, all the cottages are named after fishing flys: Dusty Miller, Naymacush, Yellow May, etc.

Our stay coincided with some heavy rain so we deeply appreciated the beautiful, cavernous lakeside recreation hall. Framed with full

A guest cottage.

timbers, with a soaring barn ceiling, it encloses a full-size shuffle-board court, an ornate old upright piano, table tennis, and ample stocks of children's toys, games, and art supplies.

For swimming guests turn to Big Averill Lake, an all-but-unpopulated 1,200-acre body of water about a mile's walk through the woods from the main lodge. Quimby owns about a quarter of the shoreline. The walk, on a wide, relatively level path, is pretty and posed no challenge for our school-age children. Younger children can ride over with their parents on the resort's electric cart.

The beach here has a small sandy area flanked by broad rocks, one of which is perfect for stretching out and sunbathing. Behind this is a lawn with several picnic tables. You can bring a picnic lunch down here in lieu of eating in the dining room (the lunch is a basket or knapsack containing sandwiches, relishes, a hot or cold beverage, cookies, and fruit). Back toward the woods is a beach recreation house and a pair of privies. Down the shore a bit from the swimming area is a boat dock with canoes, rowboats, Sunfish, and windsurfers. A float with a diving board is anchored offshore.

The resort also maintains a much larger sandy beach about a mile farther on around the lake. You can reach it on foot or take your car and drive the long way around the lake, a trip of perhaps 15 minutes. Here, once a week, the resort throws a big family cookout featuring tug-of-war and volleyball contests. This is only one of numerous events organized for guests during the "high season," which runs from mid-July through August.

Every day, morning and afternoon, the young recreation staff takes children aged approximately 5 and up off for an imaginative variety of adventures. Every morning the day's schedule is written on a blackboard just outside the dining room door; attendance is free and strictly optional. Events include magic shows; peanut hunts; swimming, boating, and hiking expeditions; frog-jumping contests; and arts and crafts. Every Wednesday the kids have a sleepover in the beach house (sleeping bags provided for those who don't bring their own). They make s'mores and popcorn over a bonfire before retiring to the house for ghost stories and, perhaps, some actual sleeping.

Other regularly scheduled all-family events include a welcoming Sunday night buffet and cocktail party, a weekly squaredance in the recreation building, and a Friday-night lobster cookout at the beach house picnic area. Other nights, you might find a rousing game of Pictionary or Trivial Pursuit in progress in the recreation building.

The area abounds with hiking trails, many of which are marked on a map available in the office; lots of families come here specifically for the hiking.

Meals are taken in the dining room in the main lodge, a beautiful old farmhouse with a long porch overlooking the lake. The food is bountiful and wholesome, though basic and far from gourmet quality.

The lodge also contains a cozy, wood-paneled sitting room with a pretty stone fireplace and shelves of books, old photo albums, games, and puzzles. It's fun to browse through the albums and note that the resort is little changed from the 1920s. Behind the sitting room is the office, where the Gears stand ready to assist in any way, and where you can buy snacks and sundries.

Rockywold–Deephaven Camps

P.O. Box B
Holderness, NH 03245
603-968-3313
Open June through September

Lodging: 60 cottages with 1–7 bedrooms, living room, fire-place, porch, icebox, individual dock.

Rates: Based on minimal cottage occupancy, $1,176 per week for 2 people–$2,478 for 6, AP. Children's rates beyond minimal occupancy: $49 per week under age 2, $147 per week ages 2–5, AP. Rates reduced 20 percent in mid-June, the end of August, and early September. Housekeeping only beginning the second week in September, at a deep discount.

Facilities: 8 Har-Tru tennis courts; baseball field; 2 small swimming beaches; swimming floats; library-sitting rooms; fishing boats, canoes, and Sunfishes for rent.

Family amenities: Supervised morning program for children ages 3–5; organized games and outings for children ages 6–13; babysitting available with advance notice.

When Squam Lake was cast in the title role of the film *On Golden Pond,* its pristine, rocky, serpentine shores, unpeopled islands, and sparkling waters made such an impression on moviegoers that local real estate agents were besieged with offers to pay whatever it took to secure a waterfront house there.

Alas, in spite of its size—it's New Hampshire's second largest lake—Squam has relatively few cottages, and a year or more can pass without a single property changing hands (at stratospheric prices, needless to say).

There is, however, a way for you to experience this lovely spot — if you're willing to wait your turn. Rockywold–Deephaven Camps, Squam's only resort, has operated on a peninsula on the lake's north shore since 1897. It is difficult to imagine a more quintessential rustic Yankee summer resort than this one, and its patrons apparently agree. It's not unusual to find three or four generations of a family sharing a vacation in the same cottage they've occupied for the same week every summer for the past 40 years.

Guests stay in 60 individual cottages tucked discreetly amidst ancient shorefront pines and granite outcroppings, each with its own small private dock. Built in the early part of the century, the cottages are lovingly maintained but never, never remodeled or updated. They look exactly the same as they did 60 years ago—unfinished board walls, stone fireplaces, screened porches, footed cast-iron tubs (a cabin with a shower is a prized rarity), green-painted wicker rockers. Each cottage has an ancient wood icebox replenished daily with ice blocks harvested from the lake in midwinter. There are no televisions or radios, and no private phones (though in a recent nod toward modernity, the resort has installed several "phone centers" with provision for semiprivate conversations). There's not even any formal landscaping, just whatever nature puts around, even if it's a boulder in the middle of a footpath.

Rockywold and Deephaven were originally separate camps, founded by two friends, idealistic New England gentlewomen who taught at Hampton Institute in Virginia. Until the 1960s the camps' staff was made up entirely of Hampton students and staff members, some of whose descendants now visit the resort as guests. Over the years the camps gradually merged into one entity. But each cottage is assigned to either Rockywold or Deephaven, and each section has its own main dock, library, and dining hall.

Both dining halls are soaring, rustic lakefront affairs featuring stone fireplaces tall enough to stand in and tables with legs made of tree branches, bark and all. The meals, served buffet-style, are ample

Photo by Nancy P. Metcalf

A guest cottage.

and traditional, though without much culinary distinction—roast beef, creamed potatoes, meatloaf, oatmeal, onion soup. Here, lasagna would be considered daring. There's always a tray of bread, peanut butter, and jelly for picky young eaters, and the kitchen will put up box lunches for hikers and picnickers.

There is no bar or lounge. Guests are permitted to keep alcohol in their cottages, but the management discourages large cocktail parties.

The deliberate simplicity of the facilities notwithstanding, the resort offers a fairly high level of service. If you catch a fish, the kitchen will clean it and cook it to your specifications. If you have dirty laundry, your "cottage girl"—camp talk for maid—will wash it for you in a day and return it to you neatly folded in a wicker basket. If you request it, a big-city newspaper will be waiting for you after breakfast in the office. If you want a canoe, a fishing boat, or a Sunfish, only ask and it will appear at your dock, life jackets included. Boat rentals are about the only extra-expense item; if you want, you can rent a boat and motor from a nearby marina instead.

With its eight Har-Tru courts, meticulously groomed every day, the camp attracts some serious tennis players, and accommodates them with well-organized sign-up lists and round robin tournaments. There are also occasional organized softball and volleyball games.

The White Mountains begin in earnest a 45-minute drive north from the camp, and easier day hikes and climbs can be found a few minutes from the camp gates. Every week the camp recreation staff organizes a few group hiking outings.

But the main attraction is the lake. The fishing is superb. A short boat ride takes you to wild inlets lined with beaver dams, or gravel beaches backed by primeval forests. You can swim off your dock, although families with toddlers tend to congregate at the camp's two small sandy swimming beaches. Diving floats are placed at convenient intervals along the camp's winding waterfront. The absence of lifeguards makes close parental supervision mandatory.

The age range of the guests is vast—from infants to great-grandparents—and the camp seems to absorb all of them. Preschoolers hang out at the playground, with swings, jungle gyms, and a state-of-the-art timber playscape and sandbox. Here, at a safe distance from the water, the camp offers a morning supervised play group for children ages 3–5. Older children have irregularly scheduled group hiking trips, movies, island picnics, and field days. The camp is self-contained enough that responsible children ages perhaps 9 and up can safely be allowed to roam at will with their friends.

Every week the resort organizes a squaredance in its cavernous, open-sided auditorium-dance hall. Depending on the week there may also be a talent show or costume parade. Most of the "cottage girls" are eager to earn extra money by babysitting in the evening or afternoon.

Rockywold–Deephaven Camps does no advertising—it doesn't have to. You won't even find it listed in New Hampshire tourism guides. Its return customers fill the vast majority of cabins the entire summer. To encourage this level of loyalty, the management assigns cabins on a complicated seniority system. That means newcomers may have to wait a year or two for an opening, and even then have to accept a week very early or late in the summer. But perseverance pays off: eventually, you reach the top of the waiting list and get your turn on Golden Pond.

Timberlock

Indian Lake
Sabael, NY 12864
518-648-5494
Winter address: R.R. 1, Box 630 Woodstock, VT 05091
802-457-1621
Open late June through September

Lodging: 10 cottages with 2–3 bedrooms, sitting room, deck or porch, woodstove, bath; 4 1-room cabins with bath, porch, woodstove; 7 1-room cabins with shared trail bath, porch, some with woodstove. No electricity in lodgings; each unit has wall-hung and portable propane lanterns.

Rates: Cottages and cabins with bath, $483 per adult per week; cabins without bath, $434. Children in any accommodation, ages 1–2, no charge; 2–3, $196; 4–7, $238; 8–11, $322; 12 and up, $392; all rates AP. Rates discounted first 2 weeks of season. After September 3, $57 per person per day for bathroom units and reduced services, AP.

Facilities: Lake swimming beach; rowboats, canoes, kayaks, Sunfish, Hobie Cats, windsurfers; mountain bikes; waterskiing; 4 Har-Tru tennis courts; horseback riding; adult lodge with library, games, puzzles; archery range; horseshoes; badminton, volleyball, and basketball courts.

Family amenities: Separate children's lodge with toys, table hockey, table tennis; sand toys at beach; rope swings over sand and water.

This is an exemplary rustic resort, a place run with rare intelligence for active, sophisticated guests who know exactly what they're getting into and look forward to it all year.

As Timberlock's brochure takes pains to point out, however, it is not everyone's cup of tea. The no-frills plywood cabins have no electricity, only propane lanterns; and many are served by shared bathhouses instead of private baths. Meals are taken on an open dining porch overlooking the lake, at long plank tables.

At the same time, however, Dick and Barbara Catlin, who have owned and operated Timberlock since 1964, have arranged its routines to sweep away obstructions to its guests' full enjoyment of one another as well as the natural splendors of the central Adirondacks.

For instance, every lodging contains a document called "Welcome to Timberlock," which explains everything you need to know to be comfortable here—from how to operate the lanterns to how to sign up for trail rides to whether you can feed the chipmunks (yes). The Catlins have also supplied each lodging with a "trip book," a customized guidebook that describes dozens of hikes, canoe expeditions, and day trips, complete with maps and information on how long a trip takes, how difficult it is, and whether it's suitable for children. In other words, guests have immediate and total access to the lore they'd otherwise have to acquire piecemeal over the course of several summers. In characteristic attention to detail, each book is enclosed in a Ziploc bag so it can be carried in a knapsack safe from spills and stains.

Timberlock has a beautiful but challenging physical setting on 65 acres of hills and woods spread along about a quarter mile of frontage on Indian Lake, a 15-mile-long, narrow, and sparsely developed body of water in the midst of the Adirondack preserve. The lodgings spread out along the lake on either side of the main complex of service buildings. The most distant ones are no more than a 5-minute walk from the dining room. On arrival, you park your car in a gravel lot uphill, and a camp staffer piles your gear on a handcart to take it to your cabin.

For families with young children the Catlins recommend one of the cottages with baths. Some are all on one floor and some are A-frames

Photo by Nancy P. Metcalf

The main building.

with sleeping lofts. All have a bath with a shower or tub-shower, a living area with comfortable chairs and homemade tables and shelves, a woodstove, and a screened porch or deck with a lake view. The propane wall lanterns are safe and easy to operate and throw off a surprising amount of light, more than enough to read or play a board game after dark. The bathrooms have dimmer "night light" lanterns, and each lodging also comes equipped with a bright portable lantern. Guests who think a shelf or ledge would improve a cabin are invited to use the resort's tools and wood to make one, and many have done so.

The one-room bathless cabins hold only two single beds, a chair or two and, in some, a woodstove; they are too small for families. However, older families frequently rent these for their teenage children, who find them a great adventure. The lack of plumbing, with its attendant environmental risks, means these cabins are located at the very edge of the lake, with the most unobstructed views. Each is a short walk from one of several men's and women's "trail baths" on the property. These baths contain a sink, several toilet stalls, and a separate room with a tub-shower.

Apart from naps or changes of clothes, however, guests don't spend much time in their lodgings. Timberlock's main complex of buildings serves as living room, dining room, and recreation room for children and adults, from breakfast through the evening hours. Perched on a hill above the waterfront, the complex centers around a covered porch with rows of rocking chairs overlooking a patio ringed with rustic benches and a huge stone outdoor fireplace. Guests gather here before and after meals, the adults in lively conversation while the kids frolic nearby.

Frolicking opportunities, we might add, are thoughtfully pro-vided. Kids can straddle the porch rail and play a game that involves trying to swing a metal ring attached to a string so it hooks over a nail in the porch post. Or they can run around to the back side of the building and swing on a heavy rope tied to a tall pine tree. The slight incline there makes it possible to swing high in the air with no real danger; kids do it by the hour. In any event, children above the age of 5 or 6 can and do run in packs to their hearts' content. Parents tend to take responsibility for watching whichever kids are at hand; and, unless they stray deep into the woods (unlikely) or hurl themselves into the lake unobserved, they're not apt to come to harm.

The dining room opens onto the lake on three sides. Clear plastic shades pull down in bad weather. The large, board-floored room is furnished with long, oilcloth-covered tables and refectory benches. Guests seat themselves; the only rule is that parents MUST eat with their children. This style of service guarantees that guests will get to know one another rapidly as they chat over meals. Except for a partial breakfast buffet, food is brought to the table and served family style. The cuisine is excellent and imaginative as well as abundant: thick homemade soups and stews, turkey with all the trimmings, salads composed of the freshest fruits and vegetables, homemade pastries, fancy open-face sandwiches.

The waterfront has a sandy beach with a gradual incline, with an offshore diving float. It also has "Moby Dick," a 30-foot Army surplus rubber raft anchored a few yards offshore; only strong kids can scramble aboard but, once there, have a great time rolling and jumping around its pillowy topside. Children also adore the rope swing that drops them into the water; for safety's sake, it's set up so it can't be used without adult assistance.

Flanking the swimming area are two boating areas furnished with a good-size armada of Hobie Cats, Sunfish, kayaks, windsurfers, canoes, and fishing boats. All are free except for small motorboats. Every Sunday afternoon the waterskiing is free; it's also available at a small charge at other times.

A steep walk up the hill from the main complex are Timberlock's four Har-Tru tennis courts and its riding stables. Daily trail rides are organized free for guests; lessons can be arranged for an additional charge. Every week at least one group hike is also scheduled.

And that's about it as far as organized activities go. You might say that Timberlock is militantly unorganized. However, guests here are busy all the time; most are nature lovers who take full advantage of the region's hiking, climbing, and canoeing opportunities while others make heavy use of the on-site recreational facilities. The lake itself offers many lovely destinations a short canoe paddle (or even shorter motorboat ride) away, including a couple of secluded sandy beaches.

After dinner guests linger at the main complex. Just off to one side, cantilevered out over the hillside, is a big, cathedral-ceilinged adult reading room. Brilliantly illuminated by propane chandeliers, it contains shelves of books and magazines and all manner of board games as well as a huge stone hearth. Meanwhile, a few yards away, the children are racing around in their own playhouse, an indestructable wood building furnished with table tennis, table hockey, and assorted toys and games. By 9 or 10 P.M. guests have drifted back to their cabins (bring a flashlight to navigate the pitch-dark trails) to be lulled to sleep by the sounds of the woods.

Although they cheerfully accept guests of all ages, the Catlins strongly urge parents of infants and preschoolers to think twice about coming. Navigating the steep, rugged paths is difficult for a toddler; a stroller is an impossibility. The long, unguarded water-front requires constant parental supervision, and the resort cannot guarantee babysitters (although it will do its best to find a staffer to take on an occasional job). On the other hand, this is paradise for older children. School-age youngsters will make a half-dozen friends by dinnertime the first night, and even finicky adolescents find Timberlock a stimulating, challenging place.

Twin Lake Village

RR 1, Box 680
New London, NH 03257
603-526-6460
Open late June through early September

Lodging: 14 cottages with 2–7 bedrooms, living room, full kitchen with utensils, phone, working fireplace, heat; 4 apartments with 2–3 bedrooms and refrigerators in lodge annex; 4 suites with 2 bedrooms, 1 suite with 3 bedrooms in cottage and main lodge; 23 rooms, 19 with private baths, in main lodge, cottage, and annex.

Rates: $290–$360 per person per week, AP. Children under 2, $50 per week; 2–5, less 15 percent of weekly rate.

Facilities: 9-hole par-3 golf course, clubs for rent at pro shop; 3 clay tennis courts; 3 shuffleboard courts; hiking trails; sandy lake beach; canoes, rowboats, paddleboats, sailboats; recreation hall.

Family amenities: Children's playhouse supervised 9 A.M.–noon for children ages 2–5; weekly children's dance.

The name Twin Lake Village suggests a contemporary townhouse community, sleek and uniform and, perhaps, a little soulless. Guess again, friends. This is an unpretentious, old-fashioned summer resort where the only things the airy, many-bedroomed cottages have in common are their large, inviting front porches. Its white-clapboard main lodge, with its many added wings and annexes, gives new meaning to the word "rambling." Its furnishings and

Photo courtesy of Twin Like Village

The main lodge.

decor are old and good enough to be charming, but not so priceless and ancient as to discourage their full use by guest families. And, as we shall soon see, Twin Lake Village is ideally suited for active parents with preschool-age children.

The resort's sports amenities include, most invitingly, a 9-hole par-3 golf course that stretches down the long hillside between the rambling main lodge and the lakefront. There are also three clay tennis courts and three shuffleboard courts.

Best of all, even if you have very young children, the resort has seen to it that you can actually use all these facilities. Every morning, children ages 2—5 are invited to the supervised play barn (and we mean that literally; it's housed in a converted barn). There they'll make new friends as they play with a large stock of well-worn toys, dig in a huge (5 by 12-feet) indoor sandbox or, most temptingly, run around the vast wood floor.

Every Wednesday night the resort throws a "children's dance" in its big recreation hall. Targeted at children ages 2–8, the hour-long dance includes musical chairs, Simon Says, relay races, and dances with Mom and Dad.

There are no organized activities for them, but school-age children are warmly welcomed into the resort's regular schedule of events. These include twice-weekly golf tournaments, volleyball and bingo games, tennis round-robins, and every Wednesday night a picnic lunch in a state park at nearby Mount Kearsarge. The resort maintains a list of babysitters, both resort employees and local youngsters.

Children of all ages will find much to do at the resort's large sandy beach on Little Lake Sunapee. The lake is very clean, with a wooded shoreline with many remaining undeveloped stretches. The beach is shallow and gently sloping, the perfect set-up for children not yet ready to float, much less venture into water over their heads. Most days your kids will happily play with other children they've met at the playhouse, while the parents relax on the beach, one eye cocked for the children. The lake bottom is firm and sandy. Venturesome preschoolers will enjoy jumping off the small children's float with ladder anchored a bit offshore in about 2 feet of water. Older children and adults can swim to a diving float farther out, in about 15 feet of water. Bring your own sand chair and towel; the resort provides neither.

The kids may also enjoy an outing on the lake in one of the resort's canoes, rowboats, or kayaks, yours for the taking at the boathouse a short walk from the beach, where you'll also find suitable life preservers, paddles, and cushions. For a small extra fee you can also take out small sailboats or paddleboats.

Accommodations here are spacious and comfortable. Most families stay in the enormous individual cottages, the kind your grandmother used to summer in, with big rooms, old furniture, sheer curtains, wicker rockers, pine walls, working fireplaces, and four-poster beds. The cottages all have kitchens where you can prepare infant meals or between-meal snacks. Daily maid service keeps the cottages immaculately clean. Families on tighter budgets might opt for one of the suites or apartments, where rates run considerably less. The apartments include a small refrigerator while the suites have no food facilities of any kind.

The cottages are scattered throughout the grounds, most up the hill near the main lodge, some down by the golf course and beach. If you're up the hill you may want to drive to the beach to avoid the uphill walk back, which can tire family members with foot-long legs. Otherwise, everything is within an easy walk.

Meals are served in the main building; you'll be assigned a family table at the beginning of your stay. The menu features basic American fare—baked ham, ravioli, French toast, franks and beans—with a choice of three or four entrees at each meal. You'll generally find at least one dish to appeal to all but the most picky young eaters. Portions are abundant and service is prompt enough that squirmy youngsters won't get out of hand while waiting for their food. The resort does not have a liquor license. If you want to spend the day sightseeing, the kitchen will pack a picnic lunch for your family.

The surrounding region offers several choice day trip opportunities. Dartmouth College is a short drive up I-89, and the area abounds with crafts, antiques, and specialty shops. The town of New London, around the lake from the resort, has a summer stock company, the New London Barn Playhouse.

The Tyler Place

Highgate Springs, VT 05460
802-868-3301 or 868-4291
Open late May through mid-October

Lodging: In the main inn, 12 accommodations ranging from rooms with children's sleeping alcoves to 2-room suites; all with air conditioning, electric heat, and small refrigerator. 27 individual cottages with 2–4 bedrooms, living room, kitchenette, air conditioning, and fireplace. 14 apartment units ranging from studios to 5 bedrooms; all with kitchenette and air conditioning; most with fireplace.

Rates: $80–$125 per adult per day, AP, for first 2 adults in accommodation. Children's daily AP rates: ages 2–5, $45; 6-10, $50; 11–17, $55. Infants under 2 stay free. Rates lower before June 30 and after September 1.

Facilities: Sailing and instruction; windsurfing and instruction; 6 tennis courts; canoes; fishing boats; heated lakeshore pool; volleyball; badminton; soccer; horseshoes; water polo; recreation room with pool table and table tennis; aerobics classes; waterskiing; dancing and music; evening parties.

Family amenities: Organized programs for children ages 3–17; parents' helpers and babysitters for infants and toddlers; playground; playhouse; children's dining rooms.

After more than 40 years in the business of offering highly structured vacations for families, the Tyler Place represents the state of the art. If you have a tiny infant, the resort will supply a free crib, a kitchenette for preparing formula, and as much babysitting as you care to have. If you have a sullen adolescent, it will supply a peer group, skilled counselors, and age-appropriate activities like waterskiing and volleyball.

Located on 165 waterfront acres at the very top of Lake Champlain, just south of the Canadian border, the resort consists of an inn and individual cottages, along with excellent facilities for the usual summer resort recreation.

The layout reflects the resort's history as the sort of place that grew helter-skelter over the years rather than being laid out all at once under a master plan. Cottages and lodgings of various sizes and styles are scattered about randomly and furnished freshly and cleanly with painted old furniture and chenille bedspreads, the sort you'd find in grandmother's lake cottage. That's part of the Tyler Place's charm and gives the resort a relaxed, welcoming air. Those looking for elegance and high style, however, won't find either here.

Neither is the Tyler Place suitable for families who want an intimate, private vacation. Children spend much of their day with their age-specific play groups. Adults take their meals at tables of six. If you are not prepared to socialize and make new friends, this enforced togetherness can take you aback. Our advice is to relax and be surprised by the intimacy and openness people sometimes achieve away from their everyday social and occupational roles.

The Tyler family strongly suggests that families spend exactly one week at the resort. Arrivals and departures normally occur on Saturdays, and turnover is usually complete. Because guests—both child and adult—grow very close over the week, those who stay over for a second week often find themselves dispirited when their newfound friends have gone. This is the sort of place where families book the same week year after year and form longstanding friendships.

Depending on your taste and family configuration, you can choose from three basic types of accommodation. The rooms in the main inn all have a separate sleeping area for children so the parents can stay up later in privacy and comfort. Families with school-age children find these rooms appealing because they can enjoy the adult goings-on in the evening without having to hire babysitters. The

The dining hall.

Tylers discourage families with children 2 or younger from staying here because of the noise factor.

The cottages, all recently retrofitted with porches and French doors, are excellent for families of all ages. Some cottages are right at the water's edge, with glorious views likely to impress older children. Families with children younger than 3, however, would probably prefer the safer and grassier surroundings of the cottages set back from the water.

The 14 apartment units, in three buildings, include the resort's largest single accommodation—a five-bedroom lakeside duplex— and its most economical—units located an 8 to 10-minute walk (or 1-minute drive) from the main inn. On arrival, families are given an information packet containing the names and addresses of the other guests, and the number and ages of their children. Also included is a schedule of the week's many planned activities, which include aerobics classes, tennis matches, guided bike tours, softball games, picnics, and squaredances.

Young guests are initiated into the children's program with the Saturday evening meal. At the Tyler Place, children are required to take lunch and dinner with their age group and counselors. For breakfast they may eat with their play groups or with their parents in a separate family breakfast room. Parents wishing to lunch with their children may order picnic baskets ahead and have a picnic somewhere. Otherwise, parents eat in peace and quiet in the adults-only main dining room.

The formal children's program is intensely age-specific. Here's a brief rundown:

• Infants (newborns–age 2). Infants stay free (cribs provided), but with a condition. The resort will assign a carefully screened "parents' helper" to your family for the duration of your stay. She'll prepare meals and feed the baby, take him to play with other infants during special hours at the Midget House, the resort's nursery building for very young children, and watch him while you eat or recreate. The charge is a startlingly low $2.50–$3.50 per hour. The resort recommends a minimum of 5–6 hours of helper time per day. Or, if you prefer, you can bring your own helper from home. She can stay in your lodging at no cost (preparing her own meals, of course) beyond a $10.50 weekly "helper's fee."

•Ages 2–3. These children have a separate wing of the Midget House furnished with appropriate child-safe toys and activities and their own dining room. They get wet in sprinklers and a wading pool, take short nature walks, and otherwise follow a nursery school-type schedule of storytelling, snacks, singing, and naptime.

•Ages 4–5. This group has the main wing of the Midget House, with more complicated toys. Group activities include a wading pool and waterslide, rowing and boat rides, hayrides, soccer, kickball, and gymnastics.

•Ages 6–7. These young school-age kids eat in a children's wing of the main dining room and make use of the resort's grounds for their activities, which include swimming, boat rides, canoeing lessons, parachute games, soccer, and cookouts.

•Ages 8–10. These older grade-schoolers eat in yet another special dining room and pursue a robust activities schedule featuring, among other things, pontoon boat trips, windsurfing instruction, swimming, soccer, tennis lessons, and softball games.

•Ages 11–13. The program for these young adolescents includes waterskiing, windsurfing, swimming, pontoon boat excursions, bike and canoe trips, and all sorts of team games. Their program resumes after an early dinner in the main dining room, with lip synch contests and social interaction in the recreation room, which is equipped with video games, table tennis, and pool tables.

•Ages 14–17. This oldest group also has access to the resort's many sports and recreational facilities, as well as organized events such as canoe and bike trips, extra-late breakfasts, and movies.

Formal children's activities run from 8:30 A.M. to 1:30 P.M. Afternoons are free for spending time with parents. Evening activities begin at 5:30 P.M. and run until 8 or 9 P.M., or even later for the oldest children.

The main dining room is a large space decorated with patchwork-quilt wall hangings and polished wood floors. Meals are buffet style and the menu features good, basic country-American fare. There is a bar and wine is available with meals. On two or three nights every week the resort arranges special after-dinner adult entertainment, including a theme costume party (guests are notified of the theme in advance by mail so they can pack appropriate get-ups), a piano bar, and a Monte Carlo night.

Recreational facilities available free of charge are bicycles (one-speeders suitable for brief local trips and a limited number of 15-speed touring bikes for longer trips), windsurfers, small sailboats and rowboats, six tennis courts, and a recreation room with pool and table tennis.

Though Lake Champlain affords spectacular views and great fishing, the Tyler Place's stretch of shoreline does not really have a good swimming beach. Plan to swim in the resort's attractive, heated, lifeguarded pool right next to the lake. There is a wading pool near the main pool.

For an additional fee the resort offers adult waterskiing (teens get it free as part of their program), fishing boats with outboard motors, lake cruises, golf at a nearby country club, and indoor tennis and racquetball at a nearby sports complex.

The Tyler Place contains more than enough to keep a family occupied for a week. Those interested in day trips, however, should know that Montreal, Stowe, the Shelburne Museum of Americana, and the Long Trail are each less than an hour's drive away.

Westways on Kezar Lake

Route 5
Center Lovell, ME 04016
207-928-2663
Open year-round

Lodging: Main lodge, 7 rooms, 3 with private baths; 7 housekeeping cottages with 3–7 bedrooms, sleeping 6–14 people, many with screened porch, fireplace or woodstove.

Rates: Main lodge, $135–$195 per couple per day, MAP; $105–$165 B&B. Children under 12 sharing a room with parents, $50 MAP, $20 B&B. Cottages, $800–$1,650 per week, EP. Rates lower before July, after August. Weekly rates also available.

Facilities: 2 lake beaches; clay tennis court; fives court; fishing; canoes and sailboats; 2-lane manual pinset bowling alley; game room with billiards, library, table tennis, and piano; baseball diamond; hiking paths; ballfield.

Family amenities: Swingset-climber; children's dinner table.

Westways was once a corporate retreat for the owners and employees of the Diamond Match Company. Quite the perk it must have been when it opened in the 1920s, with private bowling alleys, good fishing, and expansive views of Kezar Lake—one of Maine's loveliest—and the mountains that surround it. Westways today is a comfortable, handsome family lake resort that remains really first-class in its facilities and service.

Photo by Steve Grant

The main lodge.

Its 100 acres on the east shore of the 9-mile-long lake allow for plenty of elbow room, enough that the resort has been expanded in recent years. Kezar has plenty of cottages around it, yet the vista from almost any point is still dominated by trees and mountains behind a rippled, reflective slab of water.

The clear, deep lake—155 feet deep in one spot—supports a wide range of gamefish, from lake trout and landlocked salmon to smallmouth bass and brook trout. Its 2,510-acre surface gives sailboaters and waterskiers plenty of room. Westways guests can use the resort's sailboats and canoes without charge. Swimmers will find the water clear and inviting.

Most families who come to Westways rent one of the privately owned cottages that are part of the resort compound. They are all large (or huge) and well-maintained, most with porches and fireplaces, some with on-premises laundry facilities. Several can sleep eight people or more, making them a real bargain for families vacationing together. And they have full access to the resort's recreational facilities. Rules on pets and smoking vary from cottage to cottage. The Westways brochure gives a full and helpful description of each.

Families with older children might also find the main lodge a suitable choice. Here each room has its own character. The large

Blue Room has antique furniture, art reproductions, and a full bath. Open the window and hear classical music wafting in from the kitchen. The West Room is decorated with fox-hunting prints and overlooks the lake.

Westways' cuisine once could have been described as country gourmet. It's now even more refined than that. However they describe it, guests will find well-prepared food served on linen-draped tables in a bright glassy room overlooking the lake. Salad dressings are fresh and tasty. Soups are varied each day. Dinner entrees range from hearty old standards like beef filet with a buttery French sauce to lower-fat choices like a nicely grilled salmon with Provençal-inspired vegetable sauce. The chef's hand with the salt-shaker is delightfully restrained.

The full-range breakfasts include fresh-cooked omelets, which, along with the robust homefries, provide plenty of fuel for a morning paddle along the shoreline.

Westways has two swimming areas. The one that lends itself best to very small children is a 2-minute walk from the main lodge. It has a protected wading area, and a few feet away is the resort's playground. Directly in front of the main lodge is a pier large enough to accommodate a few sunbathers and a youthful angler or two. A raft about 20 feet from the pier invites kids who feel comfortable in deep water.

Also near the main lodge is a beautiful boathouse. Its second story is a large, square, screened-in room furnished with wicker furniture and lovely lake views. It makes an ideal reading spot or gathering place for predinner cocktails.

Located at the western border of Maine, at the edge of the White Mountains, Westways is ideally suited for a number of appealing day excursions. North Conway, New Hampshire, with its colony of factory outlets, is only a half hour away. There is abundant hiking in the surrounding mountains. The nearby Saco River is famed among canoeists for its long stretches of sandy bottom. You can spend a blissful day floating along, stopping at intervals to dip into its stunningly clear waters.

Vacation
Villages

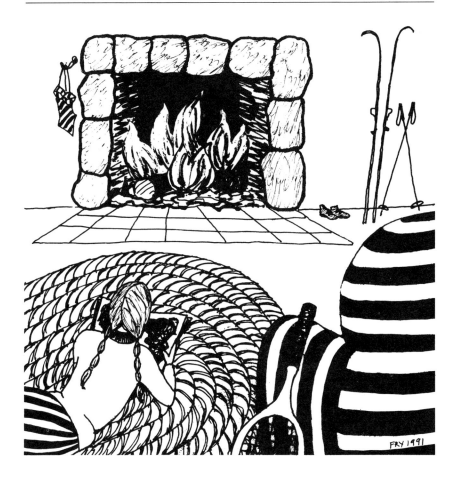

Bolton Valley Resort

Bolton Valley, VT 05477
802-434-2131 or 1-800-451-3220
Open Thanksgiving through mid-April, mid-May through mid-October

---

Lodging: 130 condominium units with 1–3 bedrooms, balcony, kitchen, deck or patio, fireplace, phone, cable TV. 146 hotel rooms; all with phone, private bath, and cable TV; some with fireplace, air conditioning, kitchen or kitchenette. Some units connect to make suites of 2–3-rooms.

Rates: $275–$358 per adult in condominium for 5-night "Vermont Vacation Package," MAP with unlimited use of recreational facilities. Same package with hotel room, $272–$459. Children's Vermont vacation package, with lodging in same room or condo as parents and day camp/nursery, $35 per day. Lodging-only rates, $484–$870 per unit per week for condo units, $70–$205 per night for hotel rooms and suites, with free use of recreational facilities. Children stay free in same room as parents. Rates higher in winter.

Facilities: Outdoor pool; indoor pool; sauna; jacuzzi; 8 all-weather tennis courts; 1 indoor court; exercise room; tanning room; trail bike rentals; nature center; hiking trails; game room with video games, table tennis, pool; restaurant; deli; gift shop; VCR and videotape rentals. Winter—6 downhill ski lifts, 43 trails, with snowmaking; 100 km cross-country ski trails; ski rentals and instruction.

Family amenities: Summer—Licensed day care nursery for infants through age 5; day camp for children ages 6–12; playground. Winter—Day care nursery; ski lessons and day care for children 5–12, including children's learn-to-ski area and ski center; list of babysitters available.

With their multimillion-dollar, high-overhead facilities in beautiful mountain settings, ski resorts are always looking for creative ways to earn money when there's no snow on the ground. Bolton Valley, located just 19 quick miles down I-89 from Burlington and Lake Champlain, has chosen to style itself a family resort in the summer. Like other such places, it offers a good vacation value for those willing to overlook the essentially wintry ambience.

Actually, Bolton Valley is misleadingly named. It sits high up in the Green Mountains, the highest elevation of any ski resort in Vermont. To get there you drive up and up and up a 4-mile-long access road to a condo-shop-hotel complex perched on the side of a mountain. The effect is dramatic and the views, wonderful.

What Bolton Valley lacks in flower gardens and charming summer buildings (the hotel and condos are in the chunky stucco-and-timber 1970s style and the landscaping is dominated by easy-to-plow, high-capacity gravel parking lots), it makes up for in the extent and generosity of its summer vacation facilities and package plans.

The Vermont Vacation Package plan, for instance, offers a family of four a total of five nights and six days in a comfortable unit, with breakfast and dinner, unlimited use of the recreational facilities, chits for off-site excursions and sports, and, for the kids, day camp or nursery care (lunch included) based at the resort's clean, modern, and well-run day care center. Total cost: under $1,200.

Families can also opt for the hotel, which has clean and stylishly decorated rooms, some of which are air conditioned and have kitchenettes for preparing lunch and snacks. These are slightly more expensive, however, and not any more conveniently located than the condos.

The day care center, like those at other ski resorts, exists principally to tend to children whose parents are on the slopes. But it works equally as well in the summer.

While many summer resorts are able to take care of children ages 3 and up, Bolton Valley's family package offers care for infants as young as 3 months. And high-quality care it is. The Honeybear Nursery, located in the main hotel complex, has a separate area for infants and 1-year-olds that's so good that resort employees (including the owner of the whole shebang) use it for year-round day care. There is a quiet, dark sleeping area and a play area with age-appropriate toys and furniture. Older preschoolers have a separate section that includes a quiet area; a rambunctious room with mats, climbers, and toys; television and VCR for movies on rainy days; and plenty of suitable games and arts materials. There's even a washer-dryer to handle spills and accidents. Lunches are prepared and served in the center's clean and modern kitchen-dining area.

On enrolling in the nursery, parents fill out a form for each child going into such details as the kind of "lovey" (a blanket, a stuffed toy) the child has, whether he uses a pacifier or bottle, etc. Babies spend almost the entire time in the nursery while older preschoolers are taken on nature walks, allowed to wade in a small pool, or turned loose in the fenced outdoor playscape.

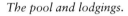

The pool and lodgings.

Photo by Nancy P. Metcalf

Older children, ages 6–12, attend Camp Bear Paw, headquartered in another part of the day-care complex. The indoor camp space is well equipped for rainy-day activities, with arts and crafts supplies and games—as well as a huge table covered with a Lego baseplate and surrounded by trays of the popular plastic bricks.

The day camp-age youngsters go much farther afield than the younger kids do. They use the entire complex for hikes, fishing trips, picnics, and games. The program includes two group tennis lessons per week. And every day, weather permitting, the kids are taken for a swim in the resort's big outdoor pool. Graduated from 3 to 6 feet deep, with a small waterslide, and framed by a brick terrace, green lawns, and woods, with a view up the hillside, it's an appealing spot for a dip. There's a good-quality wood swingset-climber nearby if the children tire of swimming.

Both the nursery and day camp are strictly optional, and parents can elect half days if they choose.

While the kids are off playing and socializing, parents, of course, have the run of the resort. Tennis players will love this place—eight outdoor courts provide plenty of playing time and space, and a resident pro runs adult and junior clinics and matches players.

In addition to unlimited use of the indoor and outdoor pools, exercise rooms, and tennis courts, the vacation package includes four "activity coupons" per adult per night of stay. These can be exchanged for on-premises activities such as tennis clinics (two coupons), or lunch at poolside (three coupons), or traded at cooperating off-site facilities. These range from a nearby 18-hole golf course (three coupons) to the Shelburne Museum of American Folk Art (four coupons) to a Lake Champlain sternwheeler cruise (three coupons).

The resort attracts lots of enthusiastic hikers and mountain bikers for good reason. It has an extensive network of trails for everyone from casual strollers to serious climbers. The nature center (in the winter it's the cross-country ski hut) will match up hikers looking for companions and provide trail maps. Take an easy stroll along Joyner Brook, which babbles fetchingly through the resort, or spend a very strenuous day hiking up to the Long Trail, and thence to the 3,640-foot summit of Bolton Mountain. The resident summer naturalist also offers a regular schedule of guided walks on which you might search for edible plants or identify some of the several hundred species of wildflowers that bloom on the premises.

Family plan guests have breakfast and dinner in the main hotel building. Depending on the house count, the restaurant can either be the smaller Lindsay's or the larger Fireside. In either case the menu is the same: a full choice of standard breakfast items, and, for dinner, a casual, eclectic menu that ought to have something for everybody—baked Brie, pasta, sandwiches, salads, soups, chicken teriyaki, and the like.

On Tuesdays the resort throws an outdoor western barbecue for MAP guests, followed by a bonfire and singalong. Thursday's the night for the New England Shore dinner. Lunches consist of burgers, fries, barbequed chicken, and sandwiches served at a poolside grill.

Don't leave Bolton Valley without exploring the lovely Burlington-Lake Champlain area. People with sweet tooths can tour (and sample the wares of) the Ben & Jerry's Ice Cream Factory or the Champlain Chocolate Factory. Fishermen can select from a number of sport-fishing charters on Lake Champlain. For a cheap thrill, ride the Lake Champlain Ferry from Burlington to Fort Kent, New York, and back again. And consult the resort's calendar for guidance to the area's many summer music, theater, crafts, and community festivals.

Hawk Inn and Mountain Resort

Route 100, P.O.Box 64
Plymouth, VT 05056
802-672-3811
Open year-round

Lodging: 50 detached houses, 25 townhouse units, 50 inn rooms; all with private bath, TV, phone. Houses and townhouse units have 2–4 bedrooms, full kitchen.

Rates: $135–$210 per room per day in inn, double occupancy, B&B, $25 per extra person in inn room; $270–$360 per unit per day for houses and townhouses. Discounts for stays of 5 nights or longer. Rates higher in winter, lower in spring. MAP available in winter for all lodgings.

Facilities: Pond swimming beach; lake marina with sailboats, canoes, Sunfish, paddleboats, rowboats, windsurfers; indoor pool; horseback riding; volleyball court; croquet; 3 outdoor tennis courts; horseshoes; nature preserve; gift shops; hiking/cross-country ski trails; pony rides; bicycles; exercise room; whirlpool; sauna; restaurant.

Family amenities: Supervised program 10 A.M.–3 P.M. daily for children ages 3–12 operating summers and school vacation weeks; video rentals; babysitting available with advance notice.

When you turn into Hawk Inn and Mountain Resort, you are immediately struck by its size. This is no bunched-together huddle of resort buildings but rather a far-flung, sophisticated community of vacation homes, most of them artfully and deliberately sited deep in the woods of the 1,176-acre property.

The many recreational facilities are equally as scattered, making a car mandatory for guests. But by the time you leave, you may well consider the resort's size and spread-out personality its biggest advantage. Hawk can accommodate hundreds of guests without feeling crowded. It effortlessly supplies total and constant privacy. You end up feeling as though the resort is there for your private use, which, in a way, it is. And, although Hawk is located—not coincidentally—within a 10-minute drive of two major downhill ski areas (Okemo and Killington), it looks, feels, and acts like a true four-season resort.

Hawk was developed and continues to present itself as an environmentally sensitive resort. Even the street names reinforce the theme, being named after raptors: Peregrine Road, Goshawk Drive, etc. There is no forest-eating golf course here, only plentiful nature trails, a lake, a pond, and lots of woods. The homes, inn, and condominium townhouses are all fashioned of natural materials and designed to blend into the woodland setting.

Hawk is a place that welcomes you and your children and makes sure, in a gentle, noncoercive way, that everyone has plenty to do. The high-quality service begins when you confirm your reservations. You'll get a preprinted grocery shopping list in the mail. Just fill in what you want, send it back, and on your arrival you'll find your cabinets and refrigerator stocked to your specifications. The charge is the price of the groceries plus 15 percent. Anyone who has ever pulled up to a housekeeping lodging at 4 P.M. with a ravenous, cranky 5-year-old in tow can well appreciate the importance of this service.

The best lodging choice for families are the resort's beautiful, secluded detached homes, which have won awards for their siting and architectural design. The homes are modern wood-and-stone affairs, with huge handmade fieldstone fireplaces, steeply sloped

A vacation home.

roofs, multiple decks, soaring ceilings, skylights, lots of windows with magnificent views, and full kitchens. Some have saunas or outdoor hot tubs. Even on overcast days the houses are light and airy. Besides the two to four bedrooms, fold-out sofas accommodate still more people. The homes are privately owned and, at their owners' option, put on the resort rental plan (roughly half the houses and townhouses on the property are on the rental plan).

For swimming you have a choice of the shallow, sandy pond beach, perfect for little kids, or the indoor pool, which older children might enjoy although the shallow end is too deep for little ones. Both places are a magnet for kids, who make friends readily in such a relaxed setting. Boating takes place on the larger Lake Amherst. Help yourself to sailboats, sailboards, canoes, paddleboats, and rowboats, or take a sailing lesson. The three tennis courts are available free of charge, and once a week Hawk offers a 1-hour workshop for beginners.

Its network of trails and scenic assets make Hawk a natural for horseback riding, and its equestrian program reflects that. There are guided 1-hour lakeside trail rides at least twice daily; intermediate and advanced riders can book longer back-country horseback excursions as well. Just before lunch children can get free, short pony rides; this event is followed by 10-minute, $5 mini-riding lessons for guests aged 5 and up. You can also, of course, book more extensive private lessons.

On weekends the celebrated Orvis fly-fishing people operate a satellite school at Hawk; you can rent the necessary equipment either for this or for do-it-yourself angling in the river, pond, or lake.

Other scheduled activities include bird walks, mountain hikes, volleyball games, and something we've never encountered anywhere else—panning for gold in Black River, which winds through the property. The staff will give you the equipment and show you how to use it, and it's no joke—nuggets turn up regularly, though, alas, they won't make much of a dent in your bill.

Hawk's day camp program is headquartered at the swimming pond and runs daily from 10 A.M. to 3 P.M., with lunch obviously included. The children are divided into the standard preschool and school-age groups and treated to age-appropriate activities—

swimming, boating, games, nature study. During this time, parents might want to visit the resort's spa for a massage or workout on the exercise equipment.

Though this is not a meal plan resort in the summer, there is a small restaurant, the River Tavern, on the premises, which serves breakfast daily and dinner from Wednesday through Sunday (Mondays and Tuesdays it offers only take-out pizza). Entrees, in the $13–$22 range, are of the veal-lamb-pasta primavera variety. From 5:30 to 7 P.M. on the nights it's open, the restaurant offers a fixed-price family menu; at $14.95 for salad, breads, entree, and dessert it's a bargain—especially when you factor in the children's menu, which offers burgers, pasta, and chicken fingers, plus potato and vegetable, in the $6–$8 range.

Our overriding sense of Hawk is one of peace and privacy. We kept finding ourselves sitting quietly in the sun, watching the children at play, or ambling along the forest trails. We left rested and wanting to return.

New Seabury

Box B
New Seabury, MA 02649
508-477-9111 or 1-800-222-2044
Open year-round

Lodging: 160 rental villas with 1–2 bedrooms, 1–2 baths, living room, kitchen or kitchenette, cable color TV, phone, deck or patio; some with air conditioning.

Rates: $210–$350 per lodging per night, EP. Rates lower before July and after September, lowest December–January. Packages covering recreational fees and some meals available except in peak summer season.

Facilities: 3-mile private ocean beach with lifeguarded swimming area; 2 heated lifeguarded outdoor pools; 2 18-hole golf courses; golf pro shop and instruction; putting greens; driving range; 16 all-weather tennis courts; tennis pro shop and instruction; 7 restaurants; specialty shops marketplace; walking-jogging trails with exercise stations; marina; rental sailboats, windsurfers; bicycle rentals; nightclubs with music and dancing.

Family amenities: Children's playground; day camp for ages 4–15; playhouse with soccer and softball fields; youth tennis instruction.

New Seabury isn't so much a resort as it is a town, a planned community meticulously laid out and built during the 1970s and 1980s to blend into the natural environment as unobtrusively as possible. The 2,000-acre property a few minutes south of the bustling commercial center of Mashpee contains about 1,500 homes and townhouses, of which only about 160 are rented out to transient guests. The rest are private vacation or year-round residences—some of them palatial indeed and all of them elegantly sited along the curving roads that wind through Cape Cod piney woods and up to oceanfront bluffs and dunes.

The abundant recreational amenities at New Seabury are scattered throughout the vast site. Visitors should plan on spending a lot of time in the car since, with the exception of one outdoor pool and a portion of the beach, no recreational facilities are within walking distance of the two townhouse villages that contain the vast majority of rental properties. The auto-oriented planners who laid out the community, however, have provided abundant and unobtrusive parking.

At any rate, moving around New Seabury is a visual pleasure: the architecture is diverse and tasteful, the natural landscape exquisite and sensitively maintained, the inevitable service facilities cleverly screened from public view. There are no ugly commercial strips here or sterile landscapes of unadorned condos.

Families visiting New Seabury can choose from two widely separated townhouse villages. Both confer access to the entire range of recreational facilities so the choice will hinge on your particular recreation preferences.

Maushop Village is perched on high sand bluffs overlooking Nantucket Sound. It's a beautiful, intimate, and clever simulation of the gray-shingled, rose-covered cottages of Nantucket itself. Though clustered in groups of as many as six attached townhouses, the units are quite private because of the ingenious placement of trellises, fences, walls, and plantings. Our unit, for instance, had a tiny brick front patio screened by a huge shore rosebush and vine-covered trellises and a back patio overlooking a common lawn but set off by the walls of the adjoining units and a white picket fence.

Families who love the ocean will probably choose Maushop. Here you can smell and see the sea as well as walk to it via several pathways and wood stairs (much of the bluff is ever-so-politely fenced off from pedestrians to protect its delicate vegetation). The

The lunch terrace.

airy villa interiors are as charming as the outsides, with their polished pine floors, floral wallpaper, chintz pillows and bed-clothes, and antique wicker or pine furnishings. Carefully designed cross-ventilation makes air conditioning unnecessary. The kitchen-ettes have dishwashers, microwaves, and plenty of dishes and cookware. All resort lodgings come with daily maid service including fresh dishtowels and potholders.

.If your party includes a golfer—or a child who would rather swim in a pool than an ocean—consider the Mews. It's very close to the two golf courses and has a large, sheltered, pretty, heated outdoor pool within an easy walk from all the villas. Children from the day camp have swimming lessons there in the mornings, but on summer afternoons it can be all but deserted. The pool has a very large shallow end and a couple of broad underwater benches which a toddler might enjoy (with parental supervision, naturally). The Mews lodgings are more California-contemporary in feel and decor but as comfortable and well-equipped as those at Maushop. They do not, however, have ocean views.

No matter where you stay, expect this to be a private resort experience. With no central dining hall or recreation building, meeting other guests is a chancy proposition.

Except for the Mews pool, water recreation centers around the New Seabury bathing beach. The handsome waterfront complex of wood buildings includes shady changing cabanas, two lunch bars where you can feast on $5 sandwich platters without changing out of your bathing suit, a heated pool with a long set of entry stairs perfect for splashing toddlers, and a sundries stand selling sunglasses, lotion, flipflops, and other beach necessaries. On a hot summer day, this is sure to be the most crowded, convivial place on the resort.

The beach itself is broad and sandy; on our visit there were lots of large rocks at the waterline, unwanted souvenirs of a hard winter. As with all beaches, this one varies according to nature's plan. Next year the rocks may well disappear. Sheltered by the offshore islands and warmed by the Gulf Stream, the surf here is tame and the water a comfortable swimming temperature.

A few hundred yards inland from the beach complex is the Poponesset Marketplace, New Seabury's "downtown," an intricate, enclosed cluster of specialty shops connected by gravel walkways shaded with overhead latticework. You can buy everything from souvenir sweatshirts to groceries to original paintings to toys. Eateries here include a pizza parlor, a raw bar, a takeout entrée emporium, an Italian café and a Ben & Jerry's. Just outside the ice-cream parlor's door is the resort's fenced, shady playscape. After dinner on warm summer nights, families congregate here to consume their Heath Bar Crunch cones and let the kids run off steam.

In the high summer season in July and August, New Seabury contracts with the YMCA to run a comprehensive children's program. Advance registration—including a health certificate—and a three-day minimum attendance are required.

SummerSalts, for 4- and 5-year-olds, operates from the Poponesset playscape for full- or optional half-day sessions. The kids get a swimming lesson, do arts and crafts, play games, and go on nature walks. The staff is maintained at a 6 to 1 ratio.

Children entering grades 1–7 start and end their day at the resort's new, barnlike recreation building, which opens out onto a soccer field and softball diamond. Subdivided into three age groups, the campers have archery, canoe, and swimming lessons as well as other day camp activities like crafts and nature study. There's an optional weekly overnight at Camp Lyndon, a sleepover YMCA camp 12 miles distant in South Sandwich. Children entering grades 3 and up can add golf and tennis lessons to their schedules.

Teen Challenge Camp participants (youngsters entering grades 8–10) are bused daily to Camp Lyndon for a demanding and exciting program of surfboarding, ropes challenge courses, climbing and rapeling, and sailing.

For adults and older children New Seabury offers state-of-the-art golf and tennis facilities. There are two 18-hole courses, one threading among houses and villas inland, and the other stretched out along a magnificent oceanfront bluff. Both begin at a luxurious clubhouse-restaurant-pro shop, where golfers will also find a couple of putting greens and a large driving range. There are daily group clinics and private lessons.

The 16-court tennis complex offers special clinics twice a week for players ages 6–12 as well as a full schedule of group and private lessons for adult players.

Smuggler's Notch

Smuggler's Notch, VT 05464
1-800-451-8752
Open year-round

Lodging: 279 rental condominiums, studio–5 bedrooms; rental condominiums, all with kitchen, bath, TV with cable and HBO, phone.

Rates: FamilyFest package from $1,079 per August week for 4-person studio to $2,155 per week for 8-person, 4-bedroom unit. Rates lower in July, lowest in June. Rates higher in winter. Most meals not included.

Facilities: Summer—2 outdoor pools; 2 waterslides; toddler pool-waterslide; village convenience store center; 4 indoor, 6 Har-Tru outdoor tennis courts; miniature golf; mountain bike rentals; hiking trails; high ropes course; horseback riding; restaurant; 2 lunch/snack bars. Winter—53 alpine ski trails on 3 mountains; 4 indoor tennis courts; 23 miles cross-country ski trails; indoor pool; sauna.

Family amenities: Day camp program for children ages 3–17 included in family package; 2 outdoor playgrounds; licensed day care center for infants through age 5; petting zoo; overnight camping trip for children 7 and up; swimming and tennis clinics; organized family games and activities; evening children's program for additional charge.

Condo complexes.

Located in a high valley surrounded on three sides by mountains, Smuggler's Notch came into being as a ski resort. Though winter's still the busy time here (with higher rates to show for it), the resort's management has gone to extraordinary lengths to make it an attractive place for families in the summer.

By and large, they've succeeded. To do so they've had to overcome a couple of significant handicaps—for one, no natural body of water on the premises except for a small mountain stream; for another, a physical plant that consists of snug, frankly wintry-looking condo units surrounded by featureless gravel parking lots of the extra-jumbo size required to hold small mountains of plowed snow.

That's the only bad news about Smuggler's. Here's the good news: one of the most comprehensive, best-organized, most imaginative children's programs we have ever seen. A dazzling variety of man-made aquatic experiences, including a 500-foot waterslide. And, perhaps most important of all, a rate structure that makes all this accessible to families of even modest means. A family of four can spend six days here, with a daily, action-packed age-appropriate program for the children and a full schedule of adult activities, for well under $1,200. Factor in the resort's location smack in the middle of the Green Mountains, an easy drive from Stowe and Burlington/Lake Champlain, and you come up with a true family vacation steal.

In the summer, Smuggler's sells its rooms as parts of various packages. Vacationing families tend to opt for the five- or seven-night FamilyFest packages featuring day camp programs for all children aged 3 and up, at no extra charge, snack and commendably nutritious lunch included.

Campers are subdivided by age. Discovery campers, ages 3–6, stick closest to home base, a day care complex that includes an expansive, well-equipped indoor playroom, a nap room, and an elaborate outdoor playground with a long hillside slide, a mazelike fort, and a pretend wood pirate ship. Campers take nature walks, visit the resort's petting zoo, fly kites, frolic in a mini-Olympics, and have a quiet storytime and nap.

The Adventure camp takes in youngsters ages 7–12. It's a physically demanding program that will use up the excess energy of even the most rambunctious kid. There are volleyball games, a session on the low part of the mountainside ropes course, visits to the pool and waterslide, and lessons in knot-tying, fire-building, and orienteering. For $15 extra the kids get an overnight hike and camping trip (Smuggler's even supplies sleeping bags).

Teenagers have an Explorer program that does its level best to interest this notoriously difficult age group. There are dancing parties, ropes course adventures, a scavenger hunt, a moonlight waterslide, volleyball games, and their own overnight. The counselors we talked to said that this program's success depends almost entirely on the personalities of the kids who show up; one bubbly, likeable youngster can energize an entire group, while an unenthusiastic one with a forceful personality can discourage everyone from participating.

For the under-3 set, Smuggler's takes full advantage of Alice's Wonderland, the state-of-the-art day care center it built to cater to the ski trade. We should have such day care centers in our own hometowns. There are separate, immaculately clean and stimulating areas for infants and toddlers. With its low staff-child ratio and lavish setting, the day care center costs extra: $32 per day or $129 for five days.

Adult programs at Smuggler's are as strenuous and well-organized as the kids' activities. Early birds can try Ti Chi Chuan, that beautiful, slow-motion Chinese calisthenics, at 7 A.M. Every morning there are hikes ranging in degree of difficulty from level walks to a strenuous climb up nearby Mount Mansfield (Vermont's highest point). Adults have their own session on the ropes course. Tennis players will find clinics, matchmaking, round robins, and team matches at the resort's excellent court complex. For $20 you can learn flycasting (gear supplied). On Sunday package-plan adult guests get a free Champagne brunch while the kids are in camp.

Every evening there's a scheduled resort-wide family activity: volleyball, a splash party, bingo, field games, bonfires, movies, marshmallow roasts. Or catch a free round of miniature golf on the brookside course.

If you want a break from cooking, the resort offers reasonably priced family fare at its restaurant. We especially liked the rooftop barbecue, served on wood picnic tables over spillproof concrete. Our youngest lost control of a full paper cup of soda without causing any lasting damage. For lunch, both pool complexes—there's one at each end of the property—have snack bars.

Off-campus, resort guests can find all the things that people go to Vermont for: scenery, charming villages, quaint antiques and crafts shops, unique restaurants, etc. One new but not-to-be-missed tourist attraction is the Ben & Jerry's ice-cream factory in nearby Waterbury. Take a tour and sample some of the newest creations of this Vermont institution.

Special Places

FRY 1991

Hotel Hershey

P.O. Box BB
Hershey, PA 17033
717-533-2171 or 1-800-HERSHEY (1-800-437-7439)
Open year-round

Lodging: 250 rooms sleeping 2–3, with private bath, cable color TV, telephones, and air conditioning. Some rooms connect into suites.

Rates: $112 per person per day, MAP; $122 per person per day, AP, double occupancy. Children's rates, ages 4 and under, no charge; 5–8, $22 per day; 9–18, $37 per day, MAP; $28 and $47 per day, AP. Rates lower before April. Variable package rates for November and December.

Facilities: Indoor and outdoor heated pools; indoor and outdoor wading pools; whirlpool; sauna; game room; putting and bowling greens; exercise room; 5 golf courses; 3 all-weather tennis courts; 5 lighted Har-Tru courts at nearby country club; indoor courts at Hershey Racquet Club; shuffleboard; riding stables; hayrides; bicycling; tobogganing; cross-country skiing; hiking and jogging trails.

Family amenities: Children's menu; in-room movies; free shuttle buses to Hersheypark, ZooAmerica North American Wildlife Park, Chocolate World, Hershey Museum of American Life; babysitting available with advance notice.

Even without the Disney-esque kid stuff of Hershey's vast amusement park, wildlife veldt, and dazzling chocolate-factory simulation, the Hotel Hershey would be worth a family visit. This magnificent, impeccably managed resort is long on old-world charm yet rich in appeal to all ages. It's also the crown jewel in an empire seeded by candy king Milton S. Hershey, who turned a sleepy eastern Pennsylvania landscape into an industrial force when he pioneered the mass production of chocolate just after the turn of the century.

Indeed, Milton Hershey kept more than 600 local construction workers busy at the height of the Great Depression, building this hotel and many of the town's other major structures. Completed in 1933, the Hotel Hershey is patterned after the grand villas of the Mediterranean—sited on high ground, its sprawling, sand-brick mission architecture overlooks the rolling countryside and distant smokestacks of the chocolate factory.

While the guest rooms have been elegantly renovated and modernized, the hotel's great public areas look as they always did. There's the Spanish-influenced Fountain Lobby with its intricate mosaics and earthy tile floors; the twin bell towers; the jutting wings that surround fragrant formal gardens and twin European reflecting pools. These latter make breathtaking mealtime views from virtually any vantage point within the great Circular Dining Room with its original stained-glass windows.

True, the Hotel Hershey has a formal way about it—especially at dinner, when men must wear jackets in the dining room and the atmosphere is charged with the crisp efficiencies of seasoned waiters and wine stewards. Here the gourmet fare is continental and can be adventurous, but the family atmosphere is likewise strong. Children are patiently attended to and provided their own excellent menu (spaghetti and meatballs, chicken, chopped sirloin, salads, soups, and desserts). On our summer weekend visit a good quarter of the tables were filled with families. But the hotel also has an informal café with a fairly wide menu and a sandwich shop where you can get hot dogs, fries, and ice cream.

Hershey, Pennsylvania's self-proclaimed reputation as the "sweetest place on earth" certainly extends to the hotel, with its ubiquitous bowls of complimentary Hershey Kisses. The familiar foil-wrapped drops also appear nightly in the guest rooms.

Eager as they may be to explore Hersheypark and its attendant attractions, children won't be bored at the hotel on rainy or lazy days. The indoor pool, for instance, is beautifully housed under a skylit roof along with a shallow children's pool and a spacious hot tub. The outdoor pool is similarly equipped, and towels are graciously provided at poolside both indoor and out. The game room includes a satisfying array of video and pinball games. Adjacent to the hotel grounds are riding stables, hard-surface tennis courts, and golf links (the hotel has its own 9-hole full-size course; and four others, including three 18-hole courses, are part of the Hershey empire and are available to hotel guests). The hotel staff do a good job of organizing rounds of shuffleboard, lawn bowling, tennis, and even hayrides to give all ages a chance to participate. You can rent bicycles as well, and in the winter slide in a toboggan or go cross-country skiing.

For a luxury grand hotel the Hotel Hershey's rates are by no means exorbitant. And one key indicator of any hotel's snootiness— its gift shop—contains surprisingly reasonably priced merchandise, from Aigner handbags and jewelry to toys, souvenirs, trifles, and patent medicines.

This attention to value carries over most importantly to Hershey's main attractions. In fact, one of the best attractions is free: the Chocolate World visitor's center, where you take an elaborate mini-tram ride, with narration and music, through a simulated chocolate factory (which gets almost uncomfortably hot during the ride through the glowing cocoa-bean roasting chamber). We found ourselves unexpectedly fascinated by the process of turning beans into chocolate liquor and then the endless stamping and extruding of Hershey bars and Kisses. At the end you get a free sample of the real thing.

The area's centerpiece attraction, however, is Hersheypark itself, a clean and bustling expanse of skyrides, aerial tramways, Ferris wheels, and roller coasters. The rides range from the lurching and looping to the mildly alarming. Small children will like the Flume,

The hotel and gardens.

which provides a thrilling, splashing waterway ride with a minimum of G-forces. Very small children are offered plenty of tame "baby" rides plus an antique, richly atmospheric carousel. There are countless carnival games, paddleboats, parades, corny-cute musical revues, and international gift shops. From the hotel the park is an easy car ride away, but we recommend using the free air-conditioned shuttle buses that stop every minute or so at the hotel's front entrance.

Park food is not only varied—from wholesome chicken, fish, and vegetable platters to gloriously nonnutritive hot dogs, ice cream, and cotton candy—but not overpriced, as food in these places so often is. You can buy lunch for a family of four for about $15.

Beyond the honky-tonk, Hershey provides plenty of more edifying fun. ZooAmerica North American Wildlife Park, adjacent to Hersheypark, is free to Hersheypark guests. Its 11 acres are stocked with flora and fauna native to the Northern Hemisphere—bison, wolves, woodland creatures, and reptiles.

Less flashy, but still worth a look, is the Hershey Museum of American Life. Its galleries chronicle the life and times of Milton Hershey but also introduce us to the domestic furnishings of the nineteenth-century Pennsylvania Dutch, artifacts of Native American life, and a new Victorian house display. Our kids' favorite item, though, was the nineteenth-century Apostolic Clock, which tells time and portrays the story of Jesus with animated figures.

Meanwhile, back at the hotel, the adjacent 23-acre Hershey Gardens contain hundreds of modern and heirloom rose hybrids and a magnificent collection of specimen trees—even a giant sequoia.

In all, the Hotel Hershey seems the most diversified way to take in what might otherwise seem a rather one-dimensional tourist mecca. The resort is strong and sophisticated enough to add an aura of adult romanticism, but all the same the kids won't feel left out.

Ridin'-Hy

Sherman Lake
Warrensburg, NY 12885
518-494-2742
Open year-round

Lodging: 12 cabins with beds and fold-out couches for 6; some with separate bedrooms. 8 rooms in main lodge with 2 double beds. 24 rooms in motel units; each with 1 double bed, 2 twin beds; 4 2-room suites with connecting bath. Private bath, phone in all lodgings.

Rates: $490–$525 per person per week, AP, with riding included. Children's weekly AP rates, with riding included, ages up to 7, $195–$225, one child under 4 stays free; 7–9, $315–$360; 10–17, $355–$395. Rates lower without horseback riding, before June, after mid-August.

Facilities: Trail and ring horseback riding; pony rides; indoor heated pool and jacuzzi; lake swimming beach; waterskiing; rowboats, paddleboats, pontoon boat; fishing; 2 all-weather tennis courts; volleyball; softball; shuffleboard; horseshoes; archery; game room with pool table, video games. Winter only—Beginner-intermediate ski slope with T-bar; snowmobiling; ice skating; horse-drawn sleigh rides; sledding.

Family amenities: Children's recreation program; morning day camp at peak periods; babysitting available with advance notice.

To say that Ridin'-Hy is a casual kind of place is to understate the degree to which kids will feel completely comfortable here. Parents may wince at the somewhat battered appearance of the lodge and its surroundings, but neither will they worry about the unruly manners or rambunctious behavior of their little ones.

Spilled milk in the dining room? A game of tag in the lobby? Toddlers in the bar? Noise, noise, noise? Just about anything goes here. In that sense, Ridin'-Hy is a true family resort. As you may have gathered by now, this is a place to indulge your children, not yourselves.

Ridin'-Hy's building and operations are in keeping with its transplanted dude-ranch motif, from the log-cabin main lodge to a menu heavy on beef and light on fresh fruits and vegetables. The lodge, chalet cabins, and single-story motel units ring a grassy courtyard that rolls down to the beach and lake. On a busy day kids swarm over the entire area, playing horseshoes, shuffleboard, basketball, tennis, baseball, and archery, and moving back and forth to the lake for a swim, paddleboat ride, or waterskiing.

If your kids have energy to burn, they can really sizzle here. The activities are varied and nonstop. Our test contingent of three boys, ages 4, 10, and 13, played a half-dozen sports daily, had a riding lesson every afternoon, a hayride at dusk, a movie after dinner, and a live rock band just before bed. The game room, complete with arcade games and a pool table, was a magnet for the older boys, who also got to waterski free of charge.

The 4-year-old would have been content to ride a pony around the courtyard all day. And he could have, if we'd let him. Two or three ponies stand tied to a tree just outside the main lodge; at any time, without extra charge, parents simply plant their kids atop the beasts and lead them around.

All three children made ample use of the lake for swimming but also, despite warm sunny weather, took frequent dips in the indoor pool and adjacent jacuzzi. There was a lifeguard on duty most of the day and evening at the pool, but parents would be wise to supervise their youngsters in the busy facility nevertheless. Even very young children can enjoy both the pool and the lake. The pool has wide

Photo courtesy of Ridin'-Hy

The main lodge.

steps at the shallow end for sitting and wading, and the lake has a sandy, gently sloping bottom.

Many guests focus almost entirely on the horseback-riding program. Lessons and trail rides are available in both the morning and afternoon for riders of all levels and abilities. You can leave a beginner for a supervised lesson in the ring while the rest of the family—even those with only minimal riding experience—go out on a trail ride in the cool Adirondack woods. The resident "cowboys" stage a live rodeo several nights a week.

The resort is open year-round, and horseback riding continues into the winter. A short beginner's ski slope, with a T-bar lift, is located just behind the horse barn. Snowmobiling, ice skating, sleigh rides, and sledding are also available.

A constant schedule of organized children's games, masquerade parties, movies, and other activities is provided year-round as well.

During the height of both winter and summer seasons, the resort offers a morning day camp for young children.

Ridin'-Hy is a favorite among school and scout groups looking for an alternative to a conventional camping trip. Accommodations certainly beat a moldy tent and the menu goes beyond baked beans, but the popularity of this place for such purposes also means you might find yourself sharing the facilities with swarms of gum-cracking teenagers, especially in the peak group-trip season in late spring and early summer.

The food at Ridin'-Hy is perhaps best appreciated by the young. While our grownup family members found the eggs and pancakes rather greasy, the 4-year-old proclaimed them the best he had ever eaten and proceeded to gorge himself. Lunches tend to be sandwiches or pasta, and dinners are meat and potatoes affairs—burgers, hot dogs, and fries.

The nearest town is Lake George Village, with its famous honky-tonk strip of tee-shirt stores, burger and pizza joints, miniature golf courses, and water parks—a great alternative to the video room on a rainy day. The Great Escape amusement park is also an easy drive away. Its location on the eastern edge of the Adirondack Park also puts Ridin'-Hy within easy reach of trout streams and excellent hiking trails.

All in all, Ridin'-Hy is not for those of refined tastes or erudite interests. But it does indeed live up to its billing—informal, economical, and eminently suitable for the boundless energies of children.

Rocking Horse Ranch

Highland, NY 12528
914-691-2927 or 1-800-647-2624
Open year-round

Lodging: 120 rooms in main lodge and Oklahoma Building; all with private bath, TV, phone; some with small refrigerator. Limited number of connecting 2-room suites.

Rates: $92–$122 per adult per night, $497–$560 per week, MAP. Children sharing room with parents, $55 per day ($259 per week) for first child, $52 ($238) for additional children, MAP. Lunch included for children under 12.

Facilities: Indoor and outdoor pools; private lake with waterskiing, fishing, paddleboats; horseback riding; hayrides; sauna; archery; rifle range; fitness room; miniature golf; 2 all-weather tennis courts; basketball court; handball court; volleyball; shuffleboard; horseshoes; croquet; putting green; indoor shooting range; bocci courts; softball field; game room with table tennis, video games, pool table; nightclub. Winter—downhill skiing; ice skating; tobogganing; sleigh rides; snowmobiles.

Family amenities: Supervised day camp; supervised evening programs; petting zoo; night patrol; playground.

Bucky Turk and his brother, Toolie, grew up poor on New York

City's Lower East Side. In the summers they trekked north to work as waiters and busboys in the resorts of the mid-Hudson Valley. Sometimes they got to work with horses. Bucky recalls fantasizing about "doing it better." In 1958 they got their chance. They bought a boarded-up hotel and set about turning it into a dude ranch.

Today, the Rocking Horse Ranch is a thriving 500-acre year-round resort where thousands of devoted customers book their rooms over a year in advance. More than 80 percent of guests are return visitors, some of them into the second or even third generation. What they get here is an activity-filled simulated cowboy experience with all the comforts of Long Island.

Most of the rooms are in the spreading, motel-modern main building, which also contains the dining room and various public rooms. Stained barnboard abounds indoors and out, and the whole place is festooned with Western paraphernalia—Native American blankets, steer skulls, old farm implements, wagon wheels. A few rooms are in the Oklahoma Building, a few steps from the main building. The clean and comfortable rooms are decorated in keeping with the theme: Southwestern-print bedspreads, ochre carpets, dark-stained wood furniture. The "Ranchette" rooms, the resort's top of the line, have sleeping space for six, a sitting area, and refrigerators.

Riding was what enchanted Bucky and Toolie into founding the ranch, and riding is what brings guests streaming up from the New York area to this day. The resort has more than 90 trained saddle horses and offers as many as six trail rides per day, depending on demand. Since there's no extra charge and no limit on how often you can ride, at peak seasons the sign-up lines can get long and tedious. An only slightly risky alternative is to go on standby a half hour or so before a ride; most times you'll get a horse.

Three or four of the ranch's two dozen experienced wranglers accompany each group. They quickly control errant mounts. Separate rides are offered for beginning, intermediate, and experienced riders, and the information booklet for arriving guests contains a full page of folksy instructions on how to handle a horse. There is no set lower age limit for the rides; the decision is based on a child's size and ability to handle a horse.

Each ride lasts about a half hour and winds through maple woods, past abandoned apple orchards, and returns along the shore of the lake. Many guests prefer winter rides through fresh snow under ice-sparkling tree branches.

Children too small for trail rides have the consolation of pony rides. And that's only the beginning of the resort's children's programs. At the day camp children ages 4–10 swim in the indoor and outdoor pools, watch kids' videos, take short hikes, and scramble on the ranch's playground, which includes two giant truck tire swings, several climbers, seesaws, and a sandbox. At the resort's petting zoo, a pair of retired horses, a llama, three goats, and a sheep are available all day for hugging and conversation.

For children ages 10–15 the program is more active and oriented toward socializing. The kids pump quarters into the machines in the video parlor, lunch on burgers and fries and shout over a blaring juke box, or play pool or table tennis. On the small lake a motorboat tows groups of kids and adults on an inflatable "banana," an activity that alternates with waterski lessons. Kids in this age group

A trail ride.

Photo courtesy of Rocking Horse Ranch

get instruction in target shooting and archery. They also enjoy joining adults in organized volleyball and softball games.

Adults have their own organized activities. The legendary Miriam has been teaching "artistic handicrafts" here for 30 years. Expect corny Catskill-style events: poolside bingo games, putting tournaments, and limbo contests.

The outdoor pool, with plenty of lounge chairs for tanning, is bordered by an outdoor snack bar that serves light lunches. The indoor pool draws children during the day; after 8 P.M. it's for adult socializing. Both pools are 3 feet at the shallow end, deep enough for kindergarteners but perhaps too deep for younger preschoolers.

Meals are served family-style at round tables. The five-course dinners generally feature beef, chicken, pasta, and fish entrees as well as a salad bar, appetizers, and a very crowded dessert bar (ice cream always included). Hamburgers and hot dogs are always available for children. Breakfast is buffet style although the kitchen is also willing to cook to order. Children get lunch at day camp while adults can eat at a cellar grill or a poolside snack bar.

The resort's activity does not stop with dinner. Every night there is some sort of adult entertainment—an adult comedian, a piano player, a country-and-western band, and a traditional Thursday night guest talent show. A "night patrol" program dispatches staffers to make regular checks of younger children sleeping in their rooms. Older children who can stay up late have their own evening activities such as "advanced" arts and crafts, a disco-and-pizza party, a bonfire-and-marshmallow roast, or sing-along. None of this bears much resemblance to the old Wyoming corral and bunkhouse, but these city slickers could care less.

Sagamore Lodge

Sagamore Road
Raquette Lake, NY 13436
315-354-5311
Open year-round

Lodging: Rooms for 75, most sleeping 2–4, in 3 lodges and 3 cottages, all with shared bath, some with fireplace.

Rates: Summer recreation weekends, $165 per adult, 2 nights, AP. Children under the age of 5 stay free; 5–12, half adult price. Winter cross-country ski weekends, $175 per adult for 2 nights, AP. Rates vary for outdoor, handcraft, history, youth, and personal development programs.

Facilities: Lake swimming area with offshore float; boathouse with canoes, Adirondack guide boats; concrete tennis court; marked hiking and cross-country ski trails.

Family amenities: Programs for families, children, and grandparents; babysitting available with advance notice.

Sagamore Lodge is not a resort. It is a piece of history being lovingly kept alive. One of the grandest surviving nineteenth-century Adirondack "great camps," today it houses a nonprofit institute that runs an imaginative series of outdoor, family, history, youth, crafts, and personal development programs open to paying members of the public. A stay at Sagamore Lodge is not a conventional vacation; it is something much more focused and—for the right kind of families—ultimately much more rewarding.

Sagamore Lodge was built between 1897 and 1899 by William West Durant, regarded as among the greatest of all constructors of the magnificent rustic camps created in the Adirondack wilderness in the late nineteenth century for wealthy Gilded-Age New Yorkers. Durant designed Sagamore Lodge as his personal residence. In 1901, beset by financial reverses, he sold it to Alfred Gwynne Vanderbilt, who used it as a vacation retreat until he went down with the Lusitania in 1915. Vanderbilt's widow, Margaret Emerson, presided over the camp for the next 40 years, much of it as one of America's best-known grand social hostesses. During her heyday, guests at the camp included celebrities like Gary Cooper, Gene Tierney, Lord Mountbatten, and Bernard Baruch.

In the 1950s Ms. Emerson donated the camp to Syracuse University, which used it as a reading school. In the 1970s, unable any longer to afford its upkeep, the university sold it to the State of New York, which, in turn, after a complicated series of transactions, kept much of the surrounding land and sold the buildings to their present owner.

Dominating the camp is the main lodge, located at the very tip of a peninsula jutting out into Sagamore Lake, a mile-long wild body of water about 4 miles south of the much larger Raquette Lake. The 3-story, chalet-style structure is sheathed in half-log siding (with the bark still attached); the immense, low-ceilinged living room features massive beams, exquisite hand-hewn rustic benches and shelving, and one of the 27 huge stone fireplaces—every one different—on the 18-acre complex.

Spread out from this main lodge are a series of outbuildings, many of them equally as large, and all built in the same rustic log, bark, and stone. Every one is a work of art; together, the effect is extraordinarily beautiful and serene.

The old laundry and servants' quarters, now called the Conference Building, serves as the complex's largest single lodging as well as its office building. Guests also stay in Wigwam, a 9-bedroom guest house perched above the rushing, boulder-strewn lake outlet; it's said that this is where Alfred Vanderbilt used to smoke cigars and play cards with his friends. Three "cottages," each with 2 vaulted log rooms, were originally built to house the Vanderbilts' grown children but are now rented out to guests.

Part of the fascination of a stay at Sagamore Lodge is in having free access to what, in fact and law, is a historical monument, the sort of place one usually gets to look at only from behind a velvet rope. The log beds were handmade by the skilled carpenters who lived and worked year-round in the complex of service buildings up the hill from the main lodge. At the top floor of the main lodge families can stay in an enormous, 5-bedded room that served as the nursery for the Vanderbilt children. Around the support posts are circular child-height tables, and just off the main room is a single room where the children's nanny presumably slept.

The tradeoff for this historical fidelity is a level of amenities that might have been grand for 1904 but that leave something to be desired in 1990. All baths are shared. Most have old-fashioned sinks with separate hot and cold spigots and big bathtubs without showers. On the other hand, the baths are as exquisitely crafted as the rest of the place, and most are the size of a small bedroom.

Families can visit Sagamore Lodge either on "recreation weekends" or as part of one of the dozens of special programs conducted there throughout the year.

The recreation weekends are the least structured programs. Participants can join the hikes led daily by the camp's staff naturalist or take in the evening lectures on Adirondack and Sagamore Lodge history, handcrafts, and architecture. In the winter activities revolve around cross-country ski tours on the network of trails that lead in all directions from the camp.

Families with the time and inclination can choose from among many suitable special programs conducted either by the institute's resident specialists or by outside resource people brought in for the occasion. Specifically geared to families are a 5-day workshop for parents and children on "building family ties" and a summer camp for grandparents and grandchildren.

Outdoors-oriented families might consider a 2-day llama trek, a fly-fishing workshop, a mountain-climbing week, or a canoe trip into the wilderness.

The many crafts and history workshops—clog dancing, rustic furniture-making, basketry, great camps tours—are too complicated for children; but, during the week, parents can hire sitters ($2 an hour for the first child, $1 for each additional child) while they

The main lodge.

attend the workshops. In good weather the children use the grounds for outdoor play; when it rains, they use the living room of the laundry building, which has a stock of suitable toys and games.

In keeping with the foundation's commitment to Sagamore Lodge's historic preservation, the recreational facilities remain as they were in the Vanderbilt-Emerson era. The lakefront swimming area is a small stretch of shoreline a few yards from the main building. There's no trucked-in sand, no lounge chairs, only a picnic table, a rope float to delineate the shallow section, and a diving raft moored offshore. The water is as cool and clean as you'd imagine a remote Adirondack lake could be.

Steps from the swimming area is Sagamore Lodge's magnificent, high-roofed, timbered boathouse. Numerous rowboats, canoes, and guideboats are here for the taking, along with life jackets of every size.

The tennis court is made of concrete and is said to play surprisingly well. The resort keeps a trunk of old racquets and balls on hand for pickup games; during our stay the large group of visiting children had a high old time with these.

Up the hill from the main residence complex is Sagamore Lodge's restored complex of service buildings, which, while not so distinguished architecturally as the main buildings, are, in many ways, an even more interesting part of the camp's history. While the Vanderbilts spent perhaps a few weeks a year at the camp, the support staff lived here year round, raising families, even operating a one-room schoolhouse.

The institute is committed to returning these buildings to their original use as much as practicable. Thus, Jackson Smith, a skilled Adirondack twig furniture maker, now works in the carpenter's building. His exquisite creations are on sale in the institute's gift shops, and visitors can drop in any time to watch him at work. A blacksmith once again labors in his shop, forging hardware to match the originals made here nearly a century ago.

Meals are taken in the original dining room, a separate building a few steps from the main lodge. It was expanded twice, once in 1901 and again in 1924 to accommodate Margaret Emerson's growing guest list. The story goes that she drew an outline of the addition in the dirt and left her workmen to figure out the rest.

Meals are served buffet style and eaten at long refectory tables. The food is basic and filling, if decidedly sub-gourmet in quality. At any rate, your spirit will be nourished by stimulating conversation with the interesting and diverse group of guests drawn to this special place.

Silver Bay
Association

Silver Bay, NY 12874
518-543-8833
Open year-round

Lodging: Main inn, 103 rooms, most with private bath, some connecting to form suites. Bayview Lodge, 27 rooms, all with private bath, some connecting to form suites. 5 other lodges, 112 rooms, all with shared bath, some with no linen service. 23 housekeeping cottages with 1–4 bedrooms, kitchen, bath, some with fireplaces, some winterized. 4 nonhousekeeping cottages with 2 bedrooms and bath. Not all units open in winter.

Rates: $75 per person per day, $452 per week, double occupancy, for inn and Bayview Lodge; $41–$63 per day, $244–$379 per week for other lodges, all rates AP. Children under 3 stay free; 3–12, one-half adult fee when sharing room with parents. Cottages, $317–$530 per unit per week, EP. Discount to guests for their first stay. Rates lower in winter.

Facilities: 2 lifeguarded lake swimming beaches; 4 red clay, 2 all-weather tennis courts; practice court; playing fields; archery range; boathouse with canoes, rowboats, rental sailboats, instruction, docking space for rent; shuffleboard; horseshoes; snack bar; crafts workshop with instruction in pottery, weaving, jewelry-making, leatherworking, stained glass, photography, silkscreening; 2 indoor gymnasiums;

weight room; library; nature center; hiking trails; watercolor instruction.

Family amenities: **Morning programs for children ages infant through high school; swimming and tennis lessons; babysitting available with advance notice.**

It took us a while to figure out what Silver Bay is, but after we did, we started to understand why its devotees have an almost religious feeling about this enormous complex on Lake George.

First you must understand that Silver Bay is not a resort in the conventional sense. It is a national conference center of the YMCA; most of its rooms are filled with people affiliated with one of the many religious and educational groups that gather here throughout the year. The 600-acre campus, with its huge and beautiful turn-of-the-century frame buildings, has the feel of a university. Religion and high moral purpose are palpable presences here; a lovely dark-shingled chapel holds center place on the grounds.

At the same time, however, Silver Bay has recreational facilities that rival (and in some cases surpass) those of any huge resort, both in quantity and quality. It has one of the choicest pieces of waterfront on the lake, taking in all of Silver Bay and parts of Bass and Oneida bays, and large expanses of flat terrain, rare for this hilly country. And, when it has rooms to spare, it gladly rents them out to vacationing families and individuals at amazingly low rates. A family of four can stay in a large room with private bath for under $1,400 a week—three meals a day, all recreation facilities, and a very elaborate day camp program included. A comfortable two-bedroom housekeeping cottage on the grounds can be had for under $500 a week, also including all recreational and children's programs but not including meals.

With prices like these, competition for lodging can get fierce. Silver Bay uses a complicated allocation system. Seniority, having donated money to Silver Bay, and having worked there, all count. Newcomers, especially those who want cottages, normally must settle for weeks early or late in the season. Among Silver Bay's loyal members are families who have racked up generations of priority.

The focal point of Silver Bay is the old inn, a massive clapboard

The main inn.

Photo by Nancy P. Metcalf

pile with a new stone-and-wood dining room attached. It looks out on the main sports complex and the lake beyond. And what a sports complex it is! Four impeccably maintained red clay tennis courts and two all-weather courts are in constant use for individual matches and group lessons. A recently rebuilt timber boathouse services a small armada of sailboats, canoes, and rowboats (you can also rent docking space for your private boat) and organizes lessons in handling them. An "equipment center" dispenses gear for what seems like every game ever invented, from shuffleboard to softball to hula hoops to lacrosse, as well as a circulating library of more than 100 board games.

Silver Bay's two swimming beaches are located well away from the marina, on the other side of the bay. Bay Beach is for serious swimmers, with marked lap lanes and a diving float, but no sandy beach area. Slim Point is better suited for young children. It has a good-sized sandy beach and a gently sloped waterfront. Lifeguards keep both places under close supervision; on busy days there are two lifeguards posted, one on shore and one on a diving float.

The children's program here is among the best we have seen. It operates every morning Monday through Friday and is staffed by professional child-care workers and teachers. After lunch break, school-age children return for a swimming lesson. The program resumes briefly after dinner, specifically so parents can attend vesper services.

Infant and preschool programs take place in the Children's Pavilion, a new and well-equipped building an easy stroll from the main inn. There are separate spaces for infants, 1- to 2-year-olds, and 3- to 5-year-olds, each furnished with appropriate toys, games, and crafts materials. Attached to the pavilion is a covered patio with easels, wood seesaws, and riding toys for the younger children. There is also a very large fenced grassy play area containing several climbers and—best of all—Silver Bay's old wood launch, with its innards removed but still equipped with steering wheel and benches as well as steps to climb in. Older preschoolers sometimes leave the enclosure for hikes or swims.

School-age children range freely about the campus going on hikes, paddling canoes, playing ball, and—for children ages 8 and up—taking an overnight camping trip. Junior high and high school youngsters have their own program, with irregular hours, centering on outdoor team-building and environmental activities.

Every week there is an evening family squaredance and a family campfire. Children old enough to do so are also welcome to participate in Silver Bay's many group hikes, boat expeditions, exercise programs, and musical entertainments.

On rainy afternoons guests of all ages flock to Silver Bay's amazing crafts workshop, a plain frame building that houses enough specialized equipment and material to equip a good-sized art school. For very modest materials fees, skilled craftspeople will instruct guests of all ages. You can throw a pot on a wheel, fashion a silver bracelet, piece together a stained glass ornament, stencil an apron or tote bag, silkscreen a poster, lace up a lanyard, tool your initials on a leather belt, or weave a doll blanket or muffler on a loom. All these activities can be geared to greater or lesser degrees of difficulty; our advice is to let the staff help decide whether your child is old enough to attempt something.

Because this is a not-for-profit institution instead of a commercial resort, Silver Bay's accommodations, even its best, are as basic as any YMCA's. The rooms in the inn and in Bayview Lodge, a stained-wood motel-type lodge about a 5-minute walk away, have plain Scandinavian-style furniture and clean, functional baths. As for the other lodges, all with shared baths, suffice it to say that they range from the ultra-basic to the downright rickety.

The cottages vary in size and style. All are clean, spacious, and comfortable, though like the hotel rooms, not luxurious. They are scattered throughout the grounds, most of them an easy walk from activities. Four small cottages, called Sunset Cottages, do not have kitchens. With two bedrooms, a bath, and a small sitting room, they are rented as American Plan hotel accommodations.

Meals are served in the big new dining hall. At each meal family groups are assigned a different table, which they will share with other guests. Hot entree choices are limited and tend toward no-frills American fare—baked chicken, steamed vegetables, lasagna, eggs and bacon, vegetable soup, crumb cake. Desserts and cold juices are served from a side buffet; salads, tea, coffee, and breads from a lazy susan at your table; and hot entrees from a cafeteria line. Silver Bay manages to orchestrate mealtimes to feed hundreds of guests reasonably promptly.

The resort is an easy drive to commercial areas along Lake George. A small gift shop and snack bar/ice cream parlor are on the grounds. But most people come to this place to rest their souls and bodies, not to shop. It somehow seems antithetical to the modest, kindly spirit of the place.

Appendixes

State by State

Serious Tennis

Also from The Countryman Press and Backcountry Publications

The Countryman Press and Backcountry Publications, long known for fine books on travel and outdoor recreation, offer a range of practical and readable guides.

Explorer's Guides from The Countryman Press

The alternative to mass-market guides with their homogenized listings. Explorer's Guides focus on independently owned inns, bed & breakfasts, and restaurants as well as on family and cultural activities reflecting the character and unique qualities of the region.

Maine: An Explorer's Guide, $16.95
New Hampshire: An Explorer's Guide, $16.95
Vermont: An Explorer's Guide, $16.95

Special Places guides from The Countryman Press

A different breed of guidebook that celebrates our regional diversity. In each volume a veteran travel writer profiles a tantalizing selection of the most interesting natural, cultural, and historical destinations in a region.

New England's Special Places, $12.95
New Jersey's Special Places, $12.95
New York State's Special Places, $12.95

Outdoor recreation guides from Backcountry Publications

Written for people of all ages and experience, these books feature detailed trail or tour directions, notes on points of interest, maps, and photographs.

Fifty Hikes in the Adirondacks, $11.95
Fifty Hikes in the White Mountains, $12.95
Pennsylvania Trout Streams and Their Hatches, $14.95
25 Bicycle Tours in Vermont, $8.95
25 Bicycle Tours in New Jersey, $9.95
Walks & Rambles in Dutchess and Putnam Counties (NY), $9.95
Waterfalls of the White Mountains, $14.95

We offer many more books on hiking, walking, bicycling, skiing, fishing, and canoeing in New England, New York State, the Mid-Atlantic states, and the Midwest—plus books on nature, rural living, New England history and humor, and many other subjects.

Our titles are available in bookshops and in many sporting goods stores, or they may be ordered directly from the publisher. When ordering by mail, please add $2.50 per order for shipping and handling. To order or obtain a complete catalog, please write The Countryman Press, Inc., P.O. Box 175, Woodstock, Vermont 05091.